Speaking CAE

Ten more practice tests for the **Cambridge C1 Advanced**

Jane Turner

PROSPERITY EDUCATION
www.prosperityeducation.net

Registered offices: Sherlock Close, Cambridge
CB3 0HP, United Kingdom

© Prosperity Education Ltd. 2024

First published 2024

ISBN: 978-1-915654-10-6

This publication is in copyright. Subject to statutory exception
and to the provisions of relevant collective licensing agreements,
no reproduction of any part may take place without the written
permission of Prosperity Education.

'Cambridge C1 Advanced' and 'CAE' are brands belonging to The Chancellor,
Masters and Scholars of the University of Cambridge and are not
associated with Prosperity Education or its products.

The moral rights of the author have been asserted in accordance with
the Copyright, Designs and Patents Act 1988.

For further information and resources, visit: www.prosperityeducation.net

To infinity and beyond.

Contents

Introduction	4
Test 1	7
Test 2	15
Test 3	23
Test 4	31
Test 5	39
Test 6	47
Test 7	55
Test 8	63
Test 9	71
Test 10	79
Model answers	Test 1	87
Examiner comments	Test 1	95

Introduction

Welcome to this edition of sample tests for the Cambridge C1 Advanced Speaking examination, which has been written to replicate the Cambridge exam experience and has undergone rigorous expert and peer review.

This section of the exam is taken in pairs, or trios, of candidates, who are assessed by two examiners: the interlocutor and the assessor. The interlocutor is responsible for delivering the instructions, handling the test booklet and interacting with the candidates, while the assessor simply listens and marks each candidate's performance.

The Speaking paper is divided into four parts, all of which comprise a different task. Different degrees of participation are expected from the candidates in each of these tasks.

In **Part 1** candidates are asked questions mainly about themselves, their background and their experiences. It starts with a set of brief introductory questions (e.g. ...*and your names are? Where are you from?*) and continues with one or more topic-based questions. These topics may include things like holidays and travel, leisure-time activities, friends and family, television, etc. In responding to these questions, candidates are expected to provide brief but complete answers.

Timing	2 minutes (pair) / 3 minutes (trio)
Focus	Giving personal information, expressing opinions about various topics, and talking about past experiences and plans for the future.
Interaction	Interlocutor – Candidate

In **Part 2** each candidate is asked to talk about two out of three photographs and also to answer a question about their partner's photographs. Each candidate must compare a pair of pictures and answer two questions about those pictures in one minute. Following this, the other candidate is asked a different question related to the pictures themselves or the topic of the pictures (thirty seconds). The three photographs and the questions are different for each candidate.

Timing	4 minutes (pair) / 6 minutes (trio)
Focus	Describing, comparing, expressing opinions and speculating.
Interaction	Interlocutor – Candidate

Part 3 is the main collaborative task of the test. In this part, candidates are presented with a topic in the form of a question (e.g. *Why might these career paths be popular at present?*) and a few prompts linked to it (e.g. healthcare, higher education, digital marketing, etc.). The candidates are then expected to develop a two-minute discussion around the topic, making use of the prompts provided. When the two minutes are up, they are asked to make a decision with regard to the topic (e.g. ...*decide which field will become most popular among young people in the near future.*). The candidates have one more minute to complete the task.

Timing	4 minutes (pair) / 6 minutes (trio)
Focus	Discussing, exchanging ideas, agreeing and disagreeing, asking for opinions, explaining views, justifying opinions, reaching agreements, making decisions, etc.
Interaction	Interlocutor – Candidate – Candidate

In **Part 4** candidates are asked some questions that stem from the discussion topic in Part 3. These are questions that normally touch on complex issues such as education, learning, work, healthy habits, careers, new technologies, etc. The candidates are expected to develop extended answers, and may be prompted to exchange views rather than answer individually.

Timing	5 minutes (pair) / 8 minutes (trio)
Focus	Exchanging ideas, extending and explaining answers, agreeing/disagreeing and justifying opinions.
Interaction	Interlocutor – Candidate – Candidate

This book aims to provide meaningful speaking practice while following the format of the C1 Advanced Speaking paper. **Model answers and examiner comments are provided for Test 1**, allowing both teachers and candidates to familiarise themselves with the format and level of the exam, and the type of questions and topics covered. Furthermore, and most importantly, students can learn, through repetitive practice, what to expect on the day of their Speaking test.

I hope that you will find this resource a useful study aid, and I wish you all the best in preparing for the examination.

Jane Turner
Cambridge, 2024

Jane Turner is an associate lecturer in EAP/EFL at Anglia Ruskin University, Cambridge, and an EFL materials writer for international exam boards, universities and publishers. She previously worked as a Cambridge ESOL examiner for the British Council, and holds an MA in Educational Management and Cambridge CELTA and DELTA.

Prosperity Education

We are an independent Publisher of resources for teachers and students of the English language. Our growing list of titles includes exam practice for the Cambridge English exams, teacher support resources, self-study student books and an expanding range for the IELTS, OET and Michigan exams.

www.prosperityeducation.net

Leave us an honest review on Amazon

We are a small publisher and so every review matters to us. We'd love for you to leave us a review on Amazon if our book has met your expectations.

Your review must be honest.

Every three months we will randomly select a lucky reviewer to receive a free book from our catalogue. Please send us a screenshot of your review to be entered into the prize draw.

Email: admin@prosperityeducaton.net

> To leave an Amazon review:
>
> 1. Go to the product detail page for the item. If you've placed an order for the item, you can also go to **Your orders**.
>
> 2. Select **Write a product review** in the **Customer Reviews** section.
>
> 3. Select a star rating. A green tick will be displayed for successfully submitted ratings.
>
> 4. Optionally, add text, photos or videos and select **Submit**.

Get the pdf of this title

Customers who purchase the print edition can avail of a 50% discount to purchase the corresponding digital version. Please email us with proof of purchase to receive this discount.

Follow us on social media

Follow us on Facebook, Instagram and YouTube for lots of free exam content and special offers. Tell your friends, colleagues or students! We randomly reward followers who share our posts.

- www.facebook.com/prosperityeducationcambridge
- www.instagram.com/prosperityeducationpublisher
- www.youtube.com/@prosperityeducation

Cambridge C1 Advanced Speaking

Test 1

Test 1 – Part 1	Cambridge C1 Advanced: Speaking
2 minutes (3 minutes for groups of three)	

Candidates' background

Good morning/afternoon/evening. My name is …………… and this is my colleague …………… .

And your names are?

Can I have your mark sheets, please?

Thank you.

First, we'd like to know something about you.

Select one or two questions and ask candidates in turn, as appropriate.

- **Where are you from?**
- **What do you do here/there?**
- **How long have you been studying English?**
- **What do you enjoy most about learning English?**

Select one or more questions from the following, as appropriate.

- **What type of entertainment do you find the most interesting? …… (Why?)**
- **What skill would you like to develop in the future? …… (Why?)**
- **What qualities would you say make you a good friend? …… (Why?)**
- **Would you describe yourself as an optimistic person? …… (Why? / Why not?)**
- **Can you tell us about an achievement that has made you very proud?**
- **If you could meet a famous person, who would you choose? …… (Why?)**
- **How important is it to you to keep up with the latest trends? …… (Why?)**
- **Who do you think has had the greatest influence on your life? …… (Why?)**

Cambridge C1 Advanced: Speaking	Test 1 – Part 2
	4 minutes (6 minutes for groups of three)

                        1 Being active   2 Shopping

Interlocutor   In this part of the test, I'm going to give each of you three photographs. I'd like you to talk about **two** of them on your own for about a minute, and also to answer a question about your partner's photographs.

(Candidate A), it's your turn first. Here are your photographs. They show **people being active**.

*Place **Part 2** booklet, open at **Task 1**, in front of Candidate A.*

I'd like you to compare **two** of the photographs, and say **what you think the people in these photos are enjoying about being active, and how these activities can help them in their daily lives.** All right?

Candidate A

1 minute

Interlocutor   Thank you. *(Candidate B)*, **what is the main factor that encourages people to be active? …… (Why?)**

Candidate B

Approximately 30 seconds

Interlocutor   Thank you. (Can I have the booklet, please?) *Retrieve **Part 2** booklet.*

Now, *(Candidate B)*, here are your photographs. They show **people doing different types of shopping.**

*Place **Part 2** booklet, open at **Task 2**, in front of Candidate B.*

I'd like you to compare **two** of the photographs, and say **why you think the people have chosen to shop in these ways, and what people should consider when shopping in these ways.**

All right?

Candidate B

1 minute

Interlocutor   Thank you. *(Candidate A)*, **which of these types of shopping is the most convenient? …… (Why?)**

Candidate A

Approximately 30 seconds

Interlocutor   Thank you. (Can I have the booklet, please?) *Retrieve **Part 2** booklet.*

What are the people enjoying about being active?
How can these activities help them in their daily lives?

Cambridge C1 Advanced: Speaking

Test 1 – Part 2
Booklet 2

Why have the people chosen to shop in these ways?
What should people consider when shopping in these ways?

Test 1 – Part 3	**Cambridge C1 Advanced: Speaking**
4 minutes (6 minutes for groups of three)	

Trying to help society

Interlocutor	Now, I'd like you to talk about something together for about two minutes *(3 minutes for groups of three).*
	Here are some ways that people sometimes choose to try and help society and a question for you to discuss. First you have some time to look at the task.
	*Place **Part 3** booklet, open at **Task 3**, in front of the candidates. Allow 15 seconds.*
	Now, talk to each other about **what might make someone reluctant to try these ways of helping society**.
Candidates	.... *2 minutes (3 minutes for groups of three)*
Interlocutor	Thank you. Now you have about a minute *(2 minutes for groups of three)* to decide **which way is most likely to make a difference to society**.
Candidates	.... *1 minute (2 minutes for groups of three)*
Interlocutor	Thank you. (Can I have the booklet, please?) *Retrieve **Part 3** booklet.*

Test 1 – Part 4	
5 minutes (8 minutes for groups of three)	

Interlocutor	*Use the following questions, in order, as appropriate:*	*Select any of the following prompts, as appropriate:*
	Do you think that everyone has a role to play in helping society? …… (Why? / Why not?)	• **What do you think?** • **Do you agree?** • **And you?**
	Some people believe that smaller, local charities achieve more than national charities. Do you agree? …… (Why? / Why not?)	
	Do you believe most people go into politics for the right reasons? …… (Why? / Why not?)	
	Some people say that the idea of 'community' is disappearing in many places. What do you think?	
	Do you think social media has a largely positive or negative impact on society? …… (Why?)	
	Some people say that it is the responsibility of governments, not charities to help society. What's your opinion?	
Interlocutor	Thank you. That is the end of the test.	

Cambridge C1 Advanced: Speaking

Test 1 – Part 3
Booklet

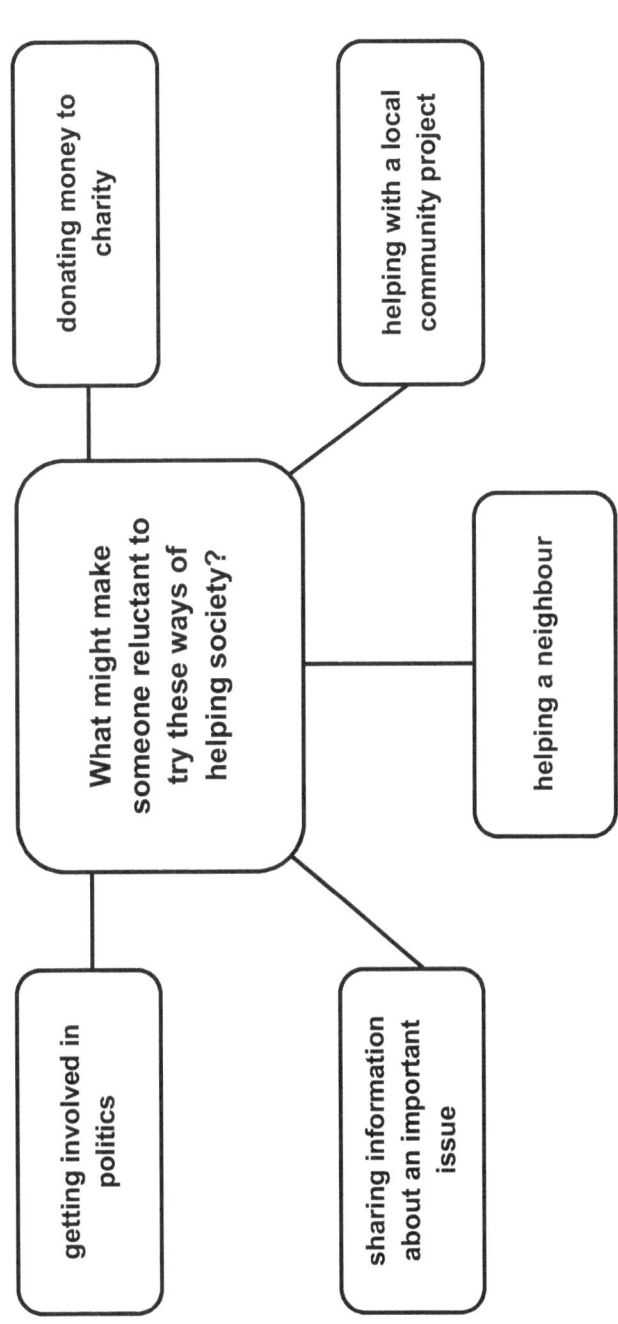

Speaking CAE — Mark sheet

Date | DD | MM | YY |

Candidate _____

Marks available

Grammatical Resource	0	1	1.5	2	2.5	3	3.5	4	4.5	5
Lexical Resource	0	1	1.5	2	2.5	3	3.5	4	4.5	5
Discourse Management	0	1	1.5	2	2.5	3	3.5	4	4.5	5
Pronunciation	0	1	1.5	2	2.5	3	3.5	4	4.5	5
Interactive Communication	0	1	1.5	2	2.5	3	3.5	4	4.5	5
Global Achievement	0	1	1.5	2	2.5	3	3.5	4	4.5	5

Item descriptors

Grammatical Resource *Control* *Range*	• Degree of control of grammatical forms. • Range of grammatical forms used.
Lexical Resource *Range* *Appropriacy*	• Range of vocabulary used to give and exchange views. • Appropriacy of vocabulary used.
Discourse Management *Extent* *Relevance* *Coherence* *Cohesion*	• Stretches of language produced. • Relevance of contributions and organisation of ideas. • Use of appropriate cohesive devices and discourse markers.
Pronunciation *Intonation* *Stress* *Individual sounds*	• Intelligibility • Intonation • Word stress • Individual sounds
Interactive Communication *Initiating* *Responding* *Development*	• Initiating, responding and linking contributions to other speakers' interventions. • Maintaining and developing interaction, and negotiating towards an outcome. • Widening the scope of the interaction.

Cambridge C1 Advanced Speaking

Test 2

Test 2 – Part 1

2 minutes (3 minutes for groups of three)

Cambridge C1 Advanced: Speaking

Candidates' background

Good morning/afternoon/evening. My name is …………… and this is my colleague …………… .

And your names are?

Can I have your mark sheets, please?

Thank you.

First, we'd like to know something about you.

Select one or two questions and ask candidates in turn, as appropriate.

- **Where are you from?**
- **What do you do here/there?**
- **How long have you been studying English?**
- **What do you enjoy most about learning English?**

Select one or more questions from the following, as appropriate.

- **Would you describe yourself as a follower or leader? …… (Why?)**
- **What sort of career do you think you are suited to? …… (Why?)**
- **Do you prefer doing active or creative activities in your free time? …… (Why?)**
- **What advice would you give to someone planning to visit your country for the first time? …… (Why?)**
- **Have you watched any interesting films or TV series recently? …… (Which ones?)**
- **If you could change anything about your home town or city, what would you change? …… (Why?)**
- **How important is it to you to set goals in life? …… (Why? / Why not?)**
- **Which aspects of your culture do you admire the most? …… (Why?)**

Cambridge C1 Advanced: Speaking	Test 2 – Part 2
	4 minutes (6 minutes for groups of three)

                         1   The arts   2   Learning about the environment

Interlocutor   In this part of the test, I'm going to give each of you three photographs. I'd like you to talk about **two** of them on your own for about a minute, and also to answer a question about your partner's photographs.

(Candidate A), it's your turn first. Here are your photographs. They show **people taking part in the arts**.

*Place **Part 2** booklet, open at **Task 1**, in front of Candidate A.*

I'd like you to compare **two** of the photographs, and say **why the people might be enjoying these activities, and how these activities might help them in their daily lives**.

All right?

Candidate A

1 minute

Interlocutor   Thank you. *(Candidate B)*, **Which of these activities do you think is the most useful? …… (Why?)**

Candidate B

Approximately 30 seconds

Interlocutor   Thank you. (Can I have the booklet, please?) *Retrieve **Part 2** booklet.*

Now, *(Candidate B)*, here are your photographs. They show **people learning about the natural world in different ways.**

*Place **Part 2** booklet, open at **Task 2**, in front of Candidate B.*

I'd like you to compare **two** of the photographs, and say **what you think the people could be learning from these activities, and how they could be feeling**.

All right?

Candidate B

1 minute

Interlocutor   Thank you. *(Candidate A)*, **Is it important to teach students about the natural world? …… (Why? / Why not?)**

Candidate A

Approximately 30 seconds

Interlocutor   Thank you. (Can I have the booklet, please?) *Retrieve **Part 2** booklet.*

What are the people enjoying about taking part in the arts?
How might the activities help the people in their daily lives?

What could the people be learning from the activities?
How might the people be feeling?

Test 2 – Part 3	**Cambridge C1 Advanced: Speaking**
4 minutes (6 minutes for groups of three)	

Leading people

Interlocutor   Now, I'd like you to talk about something together for about two minutes *(3 minutes for groups of three)*.

Here are some situations which require a leader and a question for you to discuss. First you have some time to look at the task.

*Place **Part 3** booklet, open at **Task 3**, in front of the candidates. Allow 15 seconds.*

Now, talk to each other about **the advantages and disadvantages of being a leader in these situations**.

Candidates

2 minutes (3 minutes for groups of three)

Interlocutor   Thank you. Now you have about a minute *(2 minutes for groups of three)* to decide **which situation offers the best opportunities for someone to develop leadership skills**.

Candidates

1 minute (2 minutes for groups of three)

Interlocutor   Thank you. (Can I have the booklet, please?) *Retrieve **Part 3** booklet.*

Test 2 – Part 4
5 minutes (8 minutes for groups of three)

Interlocutor   *Use the following questions, in order, as appropriate:*

Do you think that we learn enough about leading people at school? ...... (Why? / Why not?)

Some people believe that leaders should try to be friends with the people they are leading. Do you agree? ...... (Why? / Why not?)

Select any of the following prompts, as appropriate:
- **What do you think?**
- **Do you agree?**
- **And you?**

Do you believe that leaders can also be followers? ...... (Why? / Why not?)

Some people say that positive encouragement is the most effective way to lead a team. What do you think?

Is technology changing the role of a leader nowadays? ...... (How? / Why not?)

Why do you think some people are reluctant to take on leadership roles?

Interlocutor   Thank you. That is the end of the test.

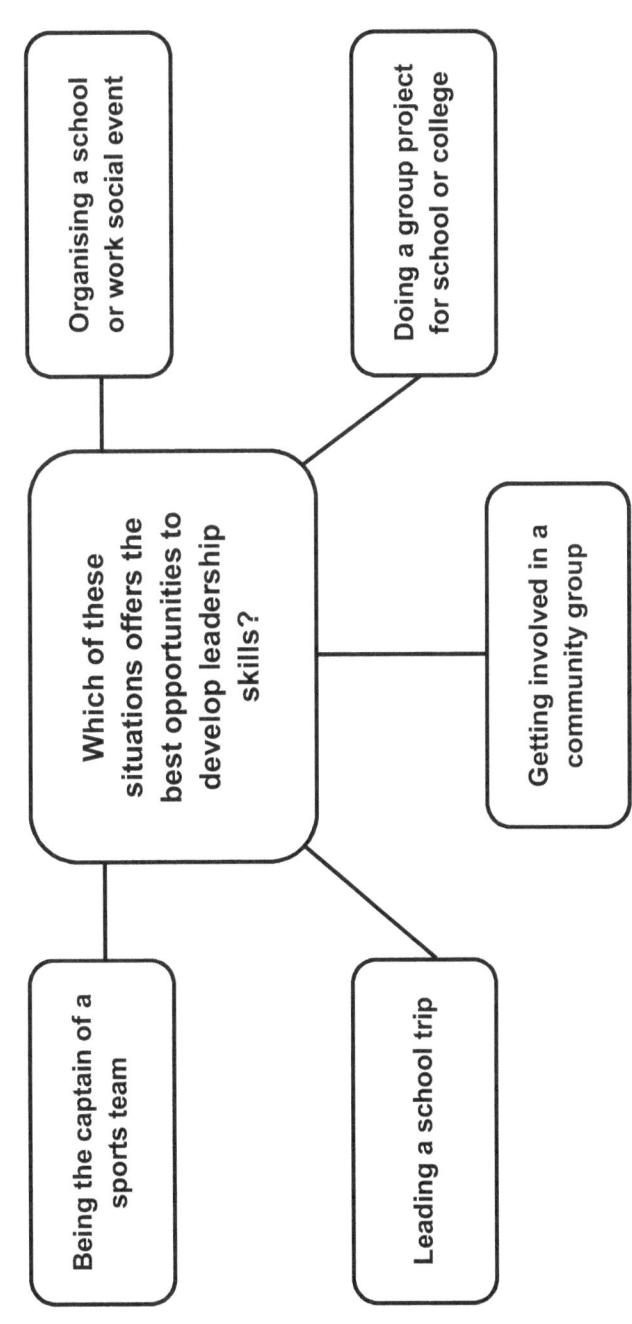

Speaking CAE — Mark sheet

Date DD MM YY   **Candidate** _____

Marks available

Grammatical Resource	0	1	1.5	2	2.5	3	3.5	4	4.5	5
Lexical Resource	0	1	1.5	2	2.5	3	3.5	4	4.5	5
Discourse Management	0	1	1.5	2	2.5	3	3.5	4	4.5	5
Pronunciation	0	1	1.5	2	2.5	3	3.5	4	4.5	5
Interactive Communication	0	1	1.5	2	2.5	3	3.5	4	4.5	5
Global Achievement	0	1	1.5	2	2.5	3	3.5	4	4.5	5

Item descriptors

Grammatical Resource *Control* *Range*	• Degree of control of grammatical forms. • Range of grammatical forms used.
Lexical Resource *Range* *Appropriacy*	• Range of vocabulary used to give and exchange views. • Appropriacy of vocabulary used.
Discourse Management *Extent* *Relevance* *Coherence* *Cohesion*	• Stretches of language produced. • Relevance of contributions and organisation of ideas. • Use of appropriate cohesive devices and discourse markers.
Pronunciation *Intonation* *Stress* *Individual sounds*	• Intelligibility • Intonation • Word stress • Individual sounds
Interactive Communication *Initiating* *Responding* *Development*	• Initiating, responding and linking contributions to other speakers' interventions. • Maintaining and developing interaction, and negotiating towards an outcome. • Widening the scope of the interaction.

Cambridge C1 Advanced Speaking

Test 3

Test 3 – Part 1
2 minutes (3 minutes for groups of three)

Cambridge C1 Advanced: Speaking

Candidates' background

Good morning/afternoon/evening. My name is …………… and this is my colleague …………… .

And your names are?

Can I have your mark sheets, please?

Thank you.

First, we'd like to know something about you.

Select one or two questions and ask candidates in turn, as appropriate.

- **Where are you from?**
- **What do you do here/there?**
- **How long have you been studying English?**
- **What do you enjoy most about learning English?**

Select one or more questions from the following, as appropriate.

- **What type of music do you like the most? …… (Why?)**
- **What places would you like to visit in the future? …… (Why?)**
- **Do you prefer you eating a home-cooked meal or eating out? …… (Why?)**
- **What helps you concentrate when you're working or studying?**
- **Have you spent time with your friends recently? …… (How?)**
- **If you could have a different daily routine, what would you change? …… (Why?)**
- **How important is it to you to do well in your career? …… (Why?)**
- **What is the best advice you've ever received? …… (Why?)**

Cambridge C1 Advanced: Speaking	Test 3 – Part 2
	4 minutes (6 minutes for groups of three)

                        1 Travel   **2 Technology**

Interlocutor   In this part of the test, I'm going to give each of you three photographs. I'd like you to talk about **two** of them on your own for about a minute, and also to answer a question about your partner's photographs.

(Candidate A), it's your turn first. Here are your photographs. They show **people travelling**.

*Place **Part 2** booklet, open at **Task 1**, in front of Candidate A.*

I'd like you to compare **two** of the photographs, and say **why you think the people have chosen to travel in this way, and how the people might be feeling**.

All right?

Candidate A

1 minute

Interlocutor   Thank you. *(Candidate B)*, **what factors have the greatest impact on people's travel choices? ...... (Why?)**

Candidate B

Approximately 30 seconds

Interlocutor   Thank you. (Can I have the booklet, please?) *Retrieve **Part 2** booklet.*

Now, *(Candidate B)*, here are your photographs. They show **people using technology in different ways.**

*Place **Part 2** booklet, open at **Task 2**, in front of Candidate B.*

I'd like you to compare **two** of the photographs, and say **how beneficial the technology is in daily life, and whether the people in the pictures might benefit from using an alternative.**

All right?

Candidate B

1 minute

Interlocutor   Thank you. *(Candidate A)*, **which of these types of technology is the most useful? ...... (Why?)**

Candidate A

Approximately 30 seconds

Interlocutor   Thank you. (Can I have the booklet, please?) *Retrieve **Part 2** booklet.*

Why might the people have chosen to travel in these ways?
How might the people be feeling?

How beneficial is this technology in daily life?
How might the people benefit from using an alternative?

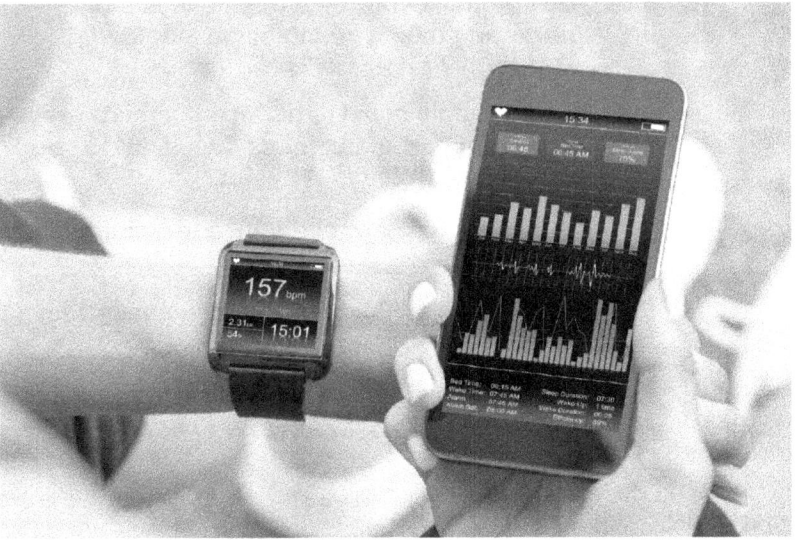

Test 3 – Part 3	Cambridge C1 Advanced: Speaking
4 minutes (6 minutes for groups of three)	

Starting a business

Interlocutor Now, I'd like you to talk about something together for about two minutes *(3 minutes for groups of three).*

Here are some of the most popular types of business that a lot of people want to start and a question for you to discuss. First you have some time to look at the task.

*Place **Part 3** booklet, open at **Task 3**, in front of the candidates. Allow 15 seconds.*

Now, talk to each other about **what people might have to consider when starting these businesses**.

Candidates

2 minutes (3 minutes for groups of three)

Interlocutor Thank you. Now you have about a minute *(2 minutes for groups of three)* to decide **what type of business is most likely to succeed**.

Candidates

1 minute (2 minutes for groups of three)

Interlocutor Thank you. (Can I have the booklet, please?) *Retrieve **Part 3** booklet.*

Test 3 – Part 4
5 minutes (8 minutes for groups of three)

Interlocutor *Use the following questions, in order, as appropriate:*

Do you think starting a business is more rewarding than working as an employee? …… (Why? / Why not?)

Some people believe that making mistakes is an important part of business success. Do you agree? …… (Why? / Why not?)

Is it better to get experience and training first or start a business as soon as you have an idea? …… (Why?)

Some people think starting a business with a friend or relative could harm their relationship. What is your opinion?

Do you think that most people have a realistic idea about what is involved in starting a business? …… (Why? / Why not?)

Select any of the following prompts, as appropriate:
- What do you think?
- Do you agree?
- And you?

Interlocutor Thank you. That is the end of the test.

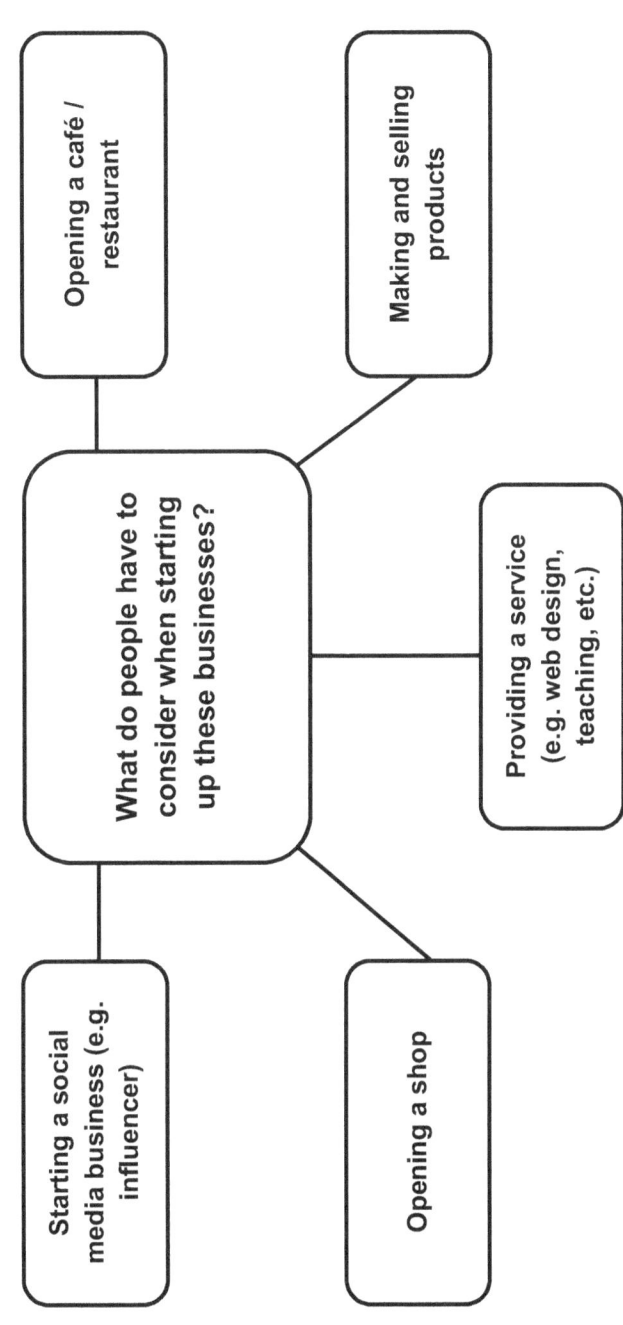

Speaking CAE — Mark sheet

| Date | DD | MM | YY | | Candidate | |

Marks available

Grammatical Resource	0	1	1.5	2	2.5	3	3.5	4	4.5	5
Lexical Resource	0	1	1.5	2	2.5	3	3.5	4	4.5	5
Discourse Management	0	1	1.5	2	2.5	3	3.5	4	4.5	5
Pronunciation	0	1	1.5	2	2.5	3	3.5	4	4.5	5
Interactive Communication	0	1	1.5	2	2.5	3	3.5	4	4.5	5
Global Achievement	0	1	1.5	2	2.5	3	3.5	4	4.5	5

Item descriptors

Grammatical Resource *Control* *Range*	• Degree of control of grammatical forms. • Range of grammatical forms used.
Lexical Resource *Range* *Appropriacy*	• Range of vocabulary used to give and exchange views. • Appropriacy of vocabulary used.
Discourse Management *Extent* *Relevance* *Coherence* *Cohesion*	• Stretches of language produced. • Relevance of contributions and organisation of ideas. • Use of appropriate cohesive devices and discourse markers.
Pronunciation *Intonation* *Stress* *Individual sounds*	• Intelligibility • Intonation • Word stress • Individual sounds
Interactive Communication *Initiating* *Responding* *Development*	• Initiating, responding and linking contributions to other speakers' interventions. • Maintaining and developing interaction, and negotiating towards an outcome. • Widening the scope of the interaction.

Cambridge C1 Advanced Speaking

Test 4

Test 4 – Part 1	Cambridge C1 Advanced: Speaking
2 minutes (3 minutes for groups of three)	

Candidates' background

Good morning/afternoon/evening. My name is …………… and this is my colleague ……………

And your names are?

Can I have your mark sheets, please?

Thank you.

First, we'd like to know something about you.

Select one or two questions and ask candidates in turn, as appropriate.

- **Where are you from?**
- **What do you do here/there?**
- **How long have you been studying English?**
- **What do you enjoy most about learning English?**

Select one or more questions from the following, as appropriate.

- **What leisure activity do you most enjoy? …… (Why?)**
- **Can you tell us about an enjoyable project you've worked on?**
- **Do you prefer to plan things in advance or live in the moment? …… (Why?)**
- **Do you think you would like to start your own business? …… (Why? / Why not?)**
- **Have you celebrated anything recently? …… (How?)**
- **If you could have a pet, which animal would you choose? …… (Why?)**
- **How important is it to you to follow cultural traditions? …… (Why?)**
- **Who do you think has had the greatest influence on your life? …… (Why?)**

Cambridge C1 Advanced: Speaking	Test 4 – Part 2
	4 minutes (6 minutes for groups of three)

1 Student life **2 Food business**

Interlocutor In this part of the test, I'm going to give each of you three photographs. I'd like you to talk about **two** of them on your own for about a minute, and also to answer a question about your partner's photographs.

(Candidate A), it's your turn first. Here are your photographs. They show **students doing different activities**.

Place Part 2 booklet, open at Task 1, in front of Candidate A.

I'd like you to compare **two** of the photographs, and say **how the students may be feeling, and whether the activities can contribute to students' personal development.**

All right?

Candidate A

1 minute

Interlocutor Thank you. *(Candidate B)*, **how important is it for students to have a range of different interests? …… (Why?)**

Candidate B

Approximately 30 seconds

Interlocutor Thank you. (Can I have the booklet, please?) *Retrieve Part 2 booklet.*

Now, *(Candidate B)*, here are your photographs. They show **people selling food in different situations**.

Place Part 2 booklet, open at Task 2, in front of Candidate B.

I'd like you to compare **two** of the photographs, and **say the most important factors to succeed in this kind of food business, and what the people could do to promote their food.**

All right?

Candidate B

1 minute

Interlocutor Thank you. *(Candidate A)*, **which of these businesses do you find most appealing? …… (Why?)**

Candidate A

Approximately 30 seconds

Interlocutor Thank you. (Can I have the booklet, please?) *Retrieve Part 2 booklet.*

How could the students be feeling?
Could the activities contribute to students' personal development?

**What are the most important factors to succeed in this kind of food business?
What could the people do to promote their food?**

Test 4 – Part 3	Cambridge C1 Advanced: Speaking
4 minutes (6 minutes for groups of three)	

Finding accommodation

Interlocutor   Now, I'd like you to talk about something together for about two minutes *(3 minutes for groups of three)*.

Here are some aspects that people may consider when finding somewhere to live and a question for you to discuss. First you have some time to look at the task.

Place Part 3 booklet, open at Task 3, in front of the candidates. Allow 15 seconds.

Now, talk to each other about **how these requirements can have an impact on people's lives.**

Candidates

2 minutes (3 minutes for groups of three)

Interlocutor   Thank you. Now you have about a minute *(2 minutes for groups of three)* to decide **which requirement is most likely to remain important over the long term.**

Candidates

1 minute (2 minutes for groups of three)

Interlocutor   Thank you. (Can I have the booklet, please?) *Retrieve Part 3 booklet.*

Test 4 – Part 4
5 minutes (8 minutes for groups of three)

Interlocutor   *Use the following questions, in order, as appropriate:*   *Select any of the following prompts, as appropriate:*

- **What do you think?**
- **Do you agree?**
- **And you?**

Is it better to prioritise the location or the property itself when choosing somewhere to live? …… (Why?)

It is sometimes said that most disputes with neighbours are due to misunderstanding. Do you agree? …… (Why? / Why not?)

What makes a neighbourhood desirable? …… (Why?)

Some people believe that students should be taught the practical skills to take care of a property. What is your opinion? …… (Why?)

Should there be a limit on the number of properties a person can own? …… (Why? / Why not?)

Some people say that moving home is one of the most stressful times in a person's life. Do you agree? …… (Why? / Why not?)

Interlocutor   Thank you. That is the end of the test.

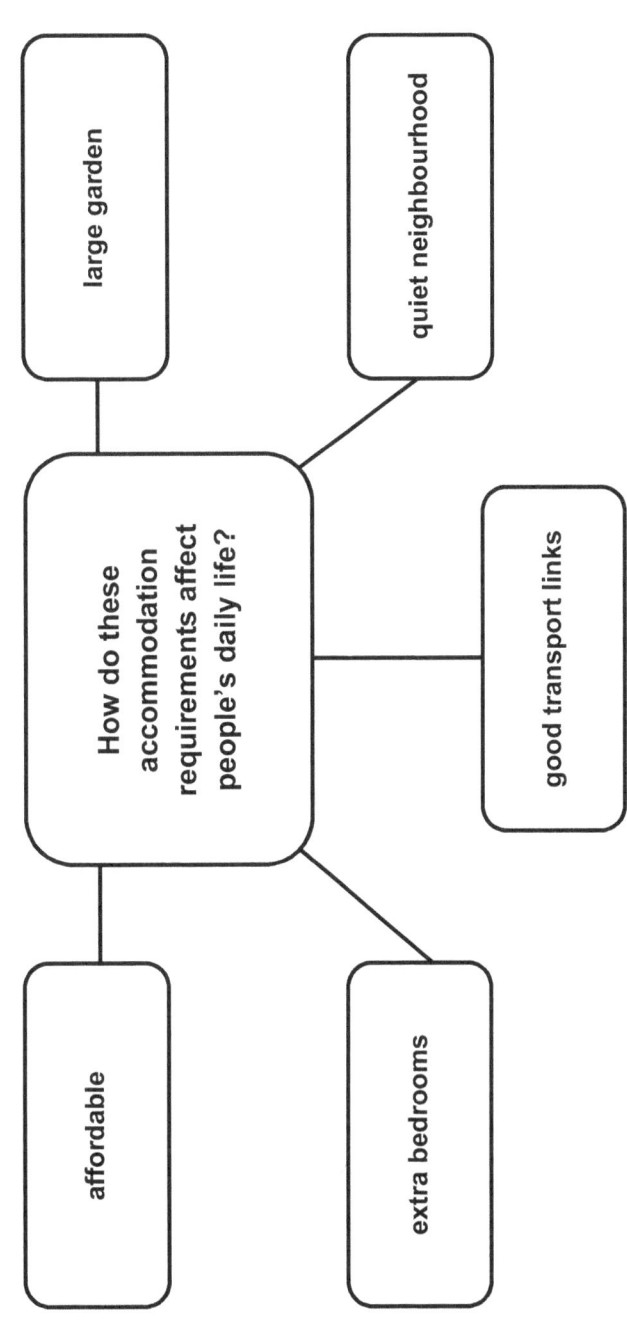

Speaking CAE — Mark sheet

Date | DD | MM | YY |

Candidate _____

Marks available

Grammatical Resource	0	1	1.5	2	2.5	3	3.5	4	4.5	5
Lexical Resource	0	1	1.5	2	2.5	3	3.5	4	4.5	5
Discourse Management	0	1	1.5	2	2.5	3	3.5	4	4.5	5
Pronunciation	0	1	1.5	2	2.5	3	3.5	4	4.5	5
Interactive Communication	0	1	1.5	2	2.5	3	3.5	4	4.5	5
Global Achievement	0	1	1.5	2	2.5	3	3.5	4	4.5	5

Item descriptors

Grammatical Resource *Control* *Range*	• Degree of control of grammatical forms. • Range of grammatical forms used.
Lexical Resource *Range* *Appropriacy*	• Range of vocabulary used to give and exchange views. • Appropriacy of vocabulary used.
Discourse Management *Extent* *Relevance* *Coherence* *Cohesion*	• Stretches of language produced. • Relevance of contributions and organisation of ideas. • Use of appropriate cohesive devices and discourse markers.
Pronunciation *Intonation* *Stress* *Individual sounds*	• Intelligibility • Intonation • Word stress • Individual sounds
Interactive Communication *Initiating* *Responding* *Development*	• Initiating, responding and linking contributions to other speakers' interventions. • Maintaining and developing interaction, and negotiating towards an outcome. • Widening the scope of the interaction.

Cambridge C1 Advanced Speaking

Test 5

| **Test 5 – Part 1** | **Cambridge C1 Advanced: Speaking** |
| 2 minutes (3 minutes for groups of three) | |

Candidates' background

Good morning/afternoon/evening. My name is .... and this is my colleague ....

And your names are?

Can I have your mark sheets, please?

Thank you.

First, we'd like to know something about you.

Select one or two questions and ask candidates in turn, as appropriate.

- **Where are you from?**
- **What do you do here/there?**
- **How long have you been studying English?**
- **What do you enjoy most about learning English?**

Select one or more questions from the following, as appropriate.

- **What's your favourite thing about taking a holiday? ...... (Why?)**
- **Would you describe yourself as an adventurous person? ...... (Why? / Why not?)**
- **Do you think you spend too much time using technology? ...... (Why? / Why not?)**
- **What advice would you give to someone thinking of studying English? ...... (Why?)**
- **Have you seen anything interesting on the internet recently? ...... (What?)**
- **If you could be extremely talented at something, what would you choose? ...... (Why?)**
- **How important is it to you to spend time in nature? ...... (Why?)**
- **Which famous person do you admire the most? ...... (Why?)**

Cambridge C1 Advanced: Speaking	**Test 5 – Part 2** 4 minutes (6 minutes for groups of three)

	1 House and home	2 Watching live sport

Interlocutor	In this part of the test, I'm going to give each of you three photographs. I'd like you to talk about **two** of them on your own for about a minute, and also to answer a question about your partner's photographs.
	(Candidate A), it's your turn first. Here are your photographs. They show **people in different types of homes**.
	*Place **Part 2** booklet, open at **Task 1**, in front of Candidate A.*
	I'd like you to compare **two** of the photographs, and say **what you think might attract people to this type of home, and how visitors might feel about spending time there**.
	All right?
Candidate A	
	.... *1 minute*
Interlocutor	Thank you. *(Candidate B)*, **which of these homes do you think offers the best quality of life? …… (Why?)**
Candidate B	
	.... *Approximately 30 seconds*
Interlocutor	Thank you. (Can I have the booklet, please?) *Retrieve **Part 2** booklet.*
	Now, *(Candidate B)*, here are your photographs. They show **people watching live sport in different ways**.
	*Place **Part 2** booklet, open at **Task 2**, in front of Candidate B.*
	I'd like you to compare **two** of the photographs, and say **why you think the people have chosen to watch sport in these ways, and the potential drawbacks of watching sport in these ways**.
	All right?
Candidate B	
	.... *1 minute*
Interlocutor	Thank you. *(Candidate A)*, **which of these ways of watching live sport has the best atmosphere? …… (Why?)**
Candidate A	
	.... *Approximately 30 seconds*
Interlocutor	Thank you. (Can I have the booklet, please?) *Retrieve **Part 2** booklet.*

Test 5 – Part 2
Booklet 1

Cambridge C1 Advanced: Speaking

What might attract people to this type of home?
How might visitors feel about spending time in this home?

Why have the people chosen to watch sport in these ways?
What are the potential drawbacks of watching sport in these ways?

Test 5 – Part 3
4 minutes (6 minutes for groups of three)

Cambridge C1 Advanced: Speaking

Life changes

Interlocutor Now, I'd like you to talk about something together for about two minutes *(3 minutes for groups of three)*.

Here are some things that people often want to change about their lives and a question for you to discuss. First you have some time to look at the task.

*Place **Part 3** booklet, open at **Task 3**, in front of the candidates. Allow 15 seconds.*

Now, talk to each other about **what people might have to consider when trying to change these areas of their life**.

Candidates

....

2 minutes (3 minutes for groups of three)

Interlocutor Thank you. Now you have about a minute *(2 minutes for groups of three)* to decide **which area is the most important to change**.

Candidates

....

1 minute (2 minutes for groups of three)

Interlocutor Thank you. (Can I have the booklet, please?) *Retrieve **Part 3** booklet.*

Test 5 – Part 4
5 minutes (8 minutes for groups of three)

Interlocutor *Use the following questions, in order, as appropriate:*

Do you think that adapting to change is a skill that can be learned? ...... (Why? / Why not?)

In your opinion, why might some people be reluctant to make major changes to improve their life?

Select any of the following prompts, as appropriate:
- What do you think?
- Do you agree?
- And you?

How important is it to seek expert advice when planning a major life change? ...... (Why?)

Some people say that making major life changes can help you develop as a person. What do you think?

Do you think that being adaptable is a desirable quality to employers? ...... (Why? / Why not?)

What are the most important signs that a major life change is worth taking? (Why?)

Interlocutor Thank you. That is the end of the test.

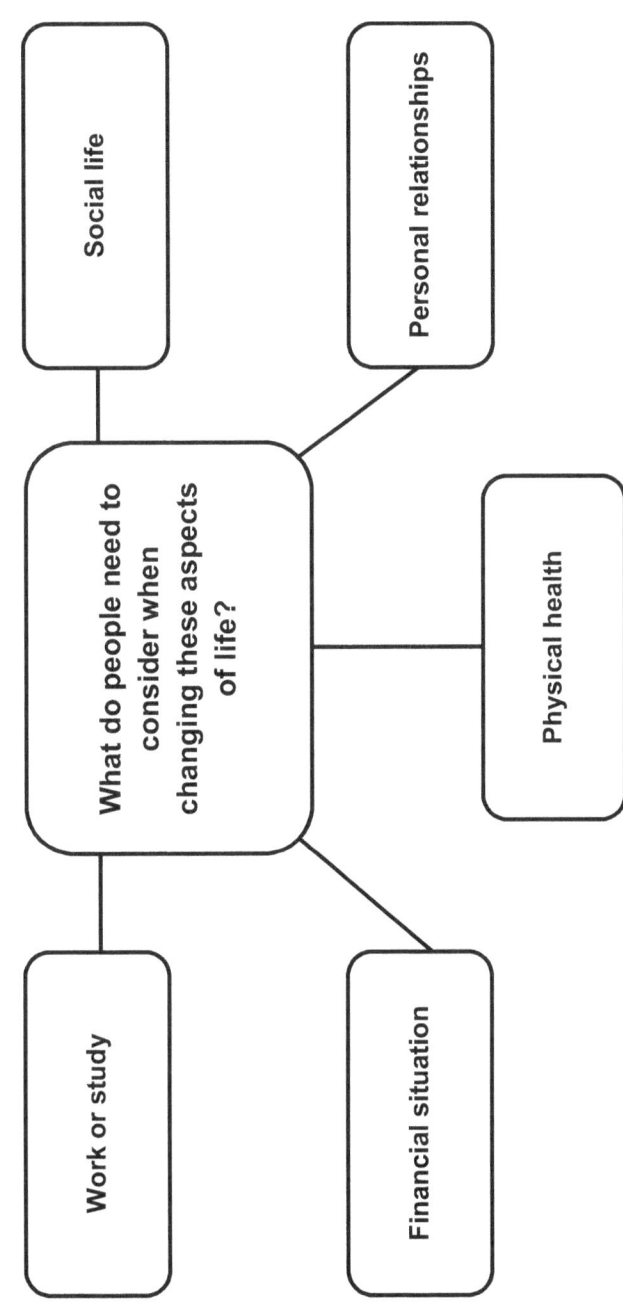

Speaking CAE — Mark sheet

Date | DD | MM | YY

Candidate _____

Marks available

Grammatical Resource	0	1	1.5	2	2.5	3	3.5	4	4.5	5
Lexical Resource	0	1	1.5	2	2.5	3	3.5	4	4.5	5
Discourse Management	0	1	1.5	2	2.5	3	3.5	4	4.5	5
Pronunciation	0	1	1.5	2	2.5	3	3.5	4	4.5	5
Interactive Communication	0	1	1.5	2	2.5	3	3.5	4	4.5	5
Global Achievement	0	1	1.5	2	2.5	3	3.5	4	4.5	5

Item descriptors

Grammatical Resource *Control* *Range*	• Degree of control of grammatical forms. • Range of grammatical forms used.
Lexical Resource *Range* *Appropriacy*	• Range of vocabulary used to give and exchange views. • Appropriacy of vocabulary used.
Discourse Management *Extent* *Relevance* *Coherence* *Cohesion*	• Stretches of language produced. • Relevance of contributions and organisation of ideas. • Use of appropriate cohesive devices and discourse markers.
Pronunciation *Intonation* *Stress* *Individual sounds*	• Intelligibility • Intonation • Word stress • Individual sounds
Interactive Communication *Initiating* *Responding* *Development*	• Initiating, responding and linking contributions to other speakers' interventions. • Maintaining and developing interaction, and negotiating towards an outcome. • Widening the scope of the interaction.

Cambridge C1 Advanced Speaking

Test 6

Test 6 – Part 1
2 minutes (3 minutes for groups of three)

Cambridge C1 Advanced: Speaking

Candidates' background

Good morning/afternoon/evening. My name is .... and this is my colleague ....

And your names are?

Can I have your mark sheets, please?

Thank you.

First, we'd like to know something about you.

Select one or two questions and ask candidates in turn, as appropriate.

- **Where are you from?**
- **What do you do here/there?**
- **How long have you been studying English?**
- **What do you enjoy most about learning English?**

Select one or more questions from the following, as appropriate.

- **What type of food do you like the most? ...... (Why?)**
- **How would you describe your dream home? ...... (Why?)**
- **Do you think you learning a language has improved your life? ...... (Why? / Why not?)**
- **Do you prefer exploring new places or returning to places you've visited before?**
- **Do you prefer late nights or early mornings? ...... (Why?)**
- **If you could swap lives with someone else for one day, what would you do? ...... (Why?)**
- **Can you tell us about a friend who has had an impact on your life? ...... (How?)**
- **What would you like to be doing in ten years? ...... (Why?)**

Cambridge C1 Advanced: Speaking	Test 6 – Part 2
	4 minutes (6 minutes for groups of three)

1 Workplaces   2 Photography

Interlocutor In this part of the test, I'm going to give each of you three photographs. I'd like you to talk about **two** of them on your own for about a minute, and also to answer a question about your partner's photographs.

(Candidate A), it's your turn first. Here are your photographs. They show **people in different types of workplace**.

*Place **Part 2** booklet, open at **Task 1**, in front of Candidate A.*

I'd like you to compare **two** of the photographs, and say **why might these workplaces have been set up in these ways, and how the people might be feeling**.

All right?

Candidate A

....

1 minute

Interlocutor Thank you. *(Candidate B)*, **which of these workplaces do you think would be the most efficient? …… (Why?)**

Candidate B

....

Approximately 30 seconds

Interlocutor Thank you. (Can I have the booklet, please?) *Retrieve **Part 2** booklet.*

Now, *(Candidate B)*, here are your photographs. They show **people involved in different types of photography**.

*Place **Part 2** booklet, open at **Task 2**, in front of Candidate B.*

I'd like you to compare **two** of the photographs, and say **why you think the people have chosen this type of photography, and what the people need to consider when doing this type of photography**.

All right?

Candidate B

....

1 minute

Interlocutor Thank you. *(Candidate A)*, **which of these types of photography requires the greatest skill? …… (Why?)**

Candidate A

....

Approximately 30 seconds

Interlocutor Thank you. (Can I have the booklet, please?) *Retrieve **Part 2** booklet.*

Why might these workplaces have been set up in these ways?
How might the people be feeling?

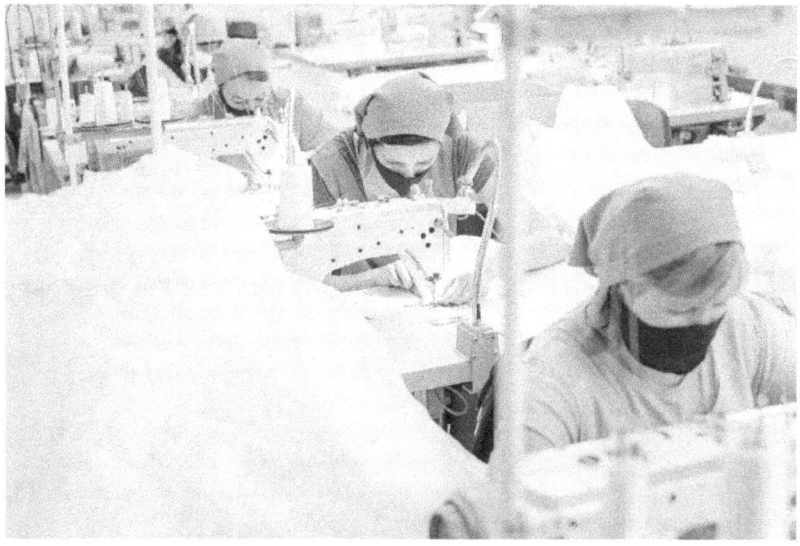

Cambridge C1 Advanced: Speaking

Test 6 – Part 2
Booklet 2

Why might the people have chosen this type of photography?
What do the people need to consider when doing this type of photography?

Test 6 – Part 3	**Cambridge C1 Advanced: Speaking**
4 minutes (6 minutes for groups of three)	

Approaches to reading

Interlocutor Now, I'd like you to talk about something together for about two minutes *(3 minutes for groups of three).*

Here are some different approaches that people might take when reading **something very long** and a question for you to discuss. First you have some time to look at the task.

Place Part 3 booklet, open at Task 3, in front of the candidates. Allow 15 seconds.

Now, talk to each other about **how these approaches can be useful when studying**.

Candidates

....

2 minutes (3 minutes for groups of three)

Interlocutor Thank you. Now you have about a minute *(2 minutes for groups of three)* to decide **which approach is most likely to make reading enjoyable**.

Candidates

....

1 minute (2 minutes for groups of three)

Interlocutor Thank you. (Can I have the booklet, please?) *Retrieve Part 3 booklet.*

Test 6 – Part 4
5 minutes (8 minutes for groups of three)

Interlocutor *Use the following questions, in order, as appropriate:*

Do you think that we study the right types of literature at school? ...... (Why? / Why not?)

Some people believe that studying literature in depth helps people appreciate books; others think it makes reading less enjoyable. What is your opinion? ...... (Why?)

In your opinion, has the development of digital technology helped or hindered the publishing industry? ...... (Why?)

Do you think that parents have a responsibility to encourage children to read? ...... (Why? / Why not?)

Why are some people reluctant to read literature?

Do you think that reading books prepares people for life? ...... (Why? / Why not?)

Select any of the following prompts, as appropriate:
- What do you think?
- Do you agree?
- And you?

Interlocutor Thank you. That is the end of the test.

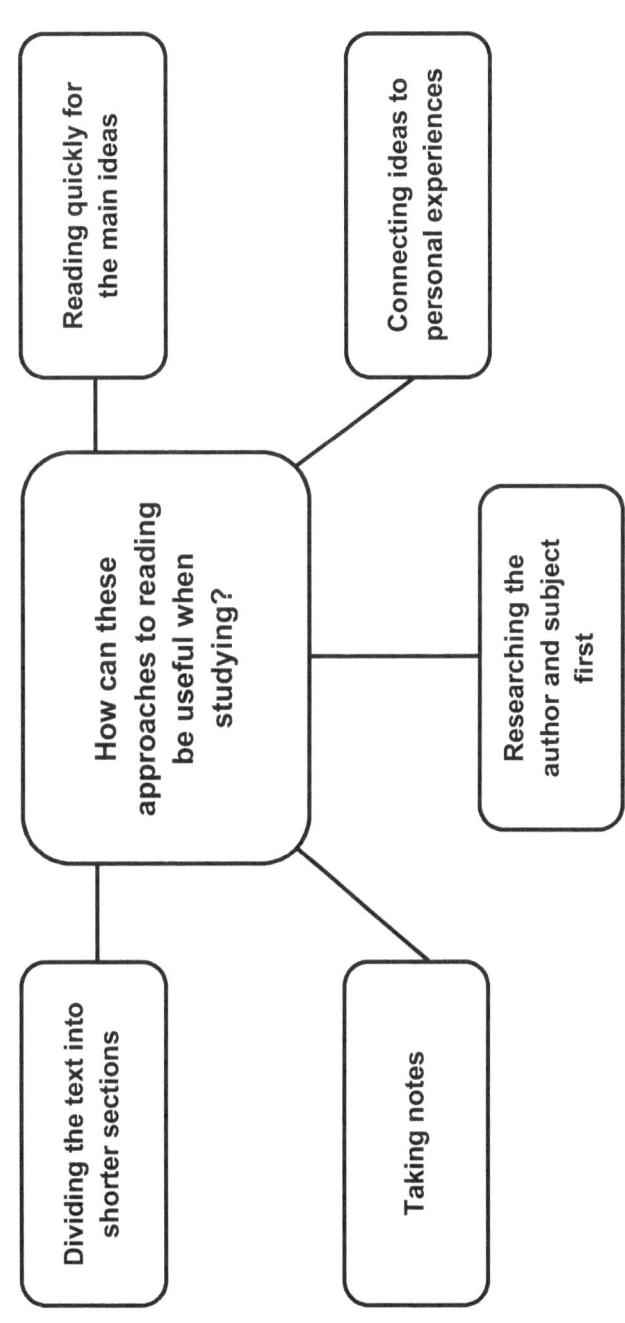

Speaking CAE — Mark sheet

Date | DD | MM | YY |

Candidate _____

Marks available

Grammatical Resource	0	1	1.5	2	2.5	3	3.5	4	4.5	5
Lexical Resource	0	1	1.5	2	2.5	3	3.5	4	4.5	5
Discourse Management	0	1	1.5	2	2.5	3	3.5	4	4.5	5
Pronunciation	0	1	1.5	2	2.5	3	3.5	4	4.5	5
Interactive Communication	0	1	1.5	2	2.5	3	3.5	4	4.5	5
Global Achievement	0	1	1.5	2	2.5	3	3.5	4	4.5	5

Item descriptors

Grammatical Resource *Control* *Range*	• Degree of control of grammatical forms. • Range of grammatical forms used.
Lexical Resource *Range* *Appropriacy*	• Range of vocabulary used to give and exchange views. • Appropriacy of vocabulary used.
Discourse Management *Extent* *Relevance* *Coherence* *Cohesion*	• Stretches of language produced. • Relevance of contributions and organisation of ideas. • Use of appropriate cohesive devices and discourse markers.
Pronunciation *Intonation* *Stress* *Individual sounds*	• Intelligibility • Intonation • Word stress • Individual sounds
Interactive Communication *Initiating* *Responding* *Development*	• Initiating, responding and linking contributions to other speakers' interventions. • Maintaining and developing interaction, and negotiating towards an outcome. • Widening the scope of the interaction.

Cambridge C1 Advanced Speaking

Test 7

Test 7 – Part 1	Cambridge C1 Advanced: Speaking
2 minutes (3 minutes for groups of three)	

Candidates' background

Good morning/afternoon/evening. My name is …………… and this is my colleague …………… .

And your names are?

Can I have your mark sheets, please?

Thank you.

First, we'd like to know something about you.

Select one or two questions and ask candidates in turn, as appropriate.

- **Where are you from?**
- **What do you do here/there?**
- **How long have you been studying English?**
- **What do you enjoy most about learning English?**

Select one or more questions from the following, as appropriate.

- **What activities do you enjoy doing with friends? …… (Why?)**
- **What is important to you when planning a day out or a trip? …… (Why?)**
- **Do you think you are good at managing your time? …… (Why? / Why not?)**
- **Does music play an important role in your life? …… (Why? / Why not?)**
- **Which means of transport do you prefer using? …… (Why?)**
- **If you could travel in time to attend a sporting event, which one would you choose? …… (Why?)**
- **How important is it to you to achieve a lot in your career? …… (Why? / Why not?)**
- **Can you tell us about a course or lesson that has inspired you? …… (How?)**

Cambridge C1 Advanced: Speaking	Test 7 – Part 2
	4 minutes (6 minutes for groups of three)

1 Gardens & outside spaces **2 Spending time with friends**

Interlocutor In this part of the test, I'm going to give each of you three photographs. I'd like you to talk about **two** of them on your own for about a minute, and also to answer a question about your partner's photographs.

(Candidate A), it's your turn first. Here are your photographs. They show **people in different types of gardens or outside spaces**.

Place Part 2 booklet, open at Task 1, in front of Candidate A.

I'd like you to compare **two** of the photographs, and say **what you think the people might enjoy about these places, and how easy these places might be to look after**.

All right?

Candidate A

1 minute

Interlocutor Thank you. *(Candidate B)*, **in which of these places are people most likely to feel relaxed? ...... (Why? / Why not?)**

Candidate B

Approximately 30 seconds

Interlocutor Thank you. (Can I have the booklet, please?) *Retrieve Part 2 booklet.*

Now, *(Candidate B)*, here are your photographs. They show **people spending time together doing different activities**.

Place Part 2 booklet, open at Task 2, in front of Candidate B.

I'd like you to compare **two** of the photographs, and say **why you think the people might have chosen to do these activities, and how they might be feeling**.

All right?

Candidate B

1 minute

Interlocutor Thank you. *(Candidate A)*, **in which situation do you think the people can most likely build a closer relationship? ...... (Why?)**

Candidate A

Approximately 30 seconds

Interlocutor Thank you. (Can I have the booklet, please?) *Retrieve Part 2 booklet.*

What might the people enjoy about these places?
How easy are these places to look after?

Why might the people have chosen to do these activities together?
How might the people be feeling?

Test 7 – Part 3	Cambridge C1 Advanced: Speaking
4 minutes (6 minutes for groups of three)	

Learning a less-popular language

Interlocutor   Now, I'd like you to talk about something together for about two minutes *(3 minutes for groups of three)*.

Here are some ways that people sometimes choose to learn a less popular language and a question for you to discuss. First you have some time to look at the task.

Place Part 3 booklet, open at Task 3, in front of the candidates. Allow 15 seconds.

Now, talk to each other about **the advantages and disadvantages of using these ways to learn a less popular language.**

Candidates

....

2 minutes (3 minutes for groups of three)

Interlocutor   Thank you. Now you have about a minute *(2 minutes for groups of three)* to decide **which method is the most likely to be effective.**

Candidates

....

1 minute (2 minutes for groups of three)

Interlocutor   Thank you. (Can I have the booklet, please?) *Retrieve Part 3 booklet.*

Test 7 – Part 4
5 minutes (8 minutes for groups of three)

Interlocutor   *Use the following questions, in order, as appropriate:*

	Select any of the following prompts, as appropriate:
Do you think that that schools should raise students' awareness of less popular languages? …… (Why? / Why not?)	• **What do you think?** • **Do you agree?** • **And you?**

Some people believe that learning about less popular languages is a waste of time. Do you agree? …… (Why? / Why not?)

Do you think that language is an important aspect of culture? …… (Why? / Why not?)

Some people say that it is important to protect all the world's languages; others argue that it is natural for some languages to die out. What do you think?

It is often said that language learning leads to personal growth. What's your opinion?

What can be done to encourage more people to learn languages? …… (Why?)

Interlocutor   Thank you. That is the end of the test.

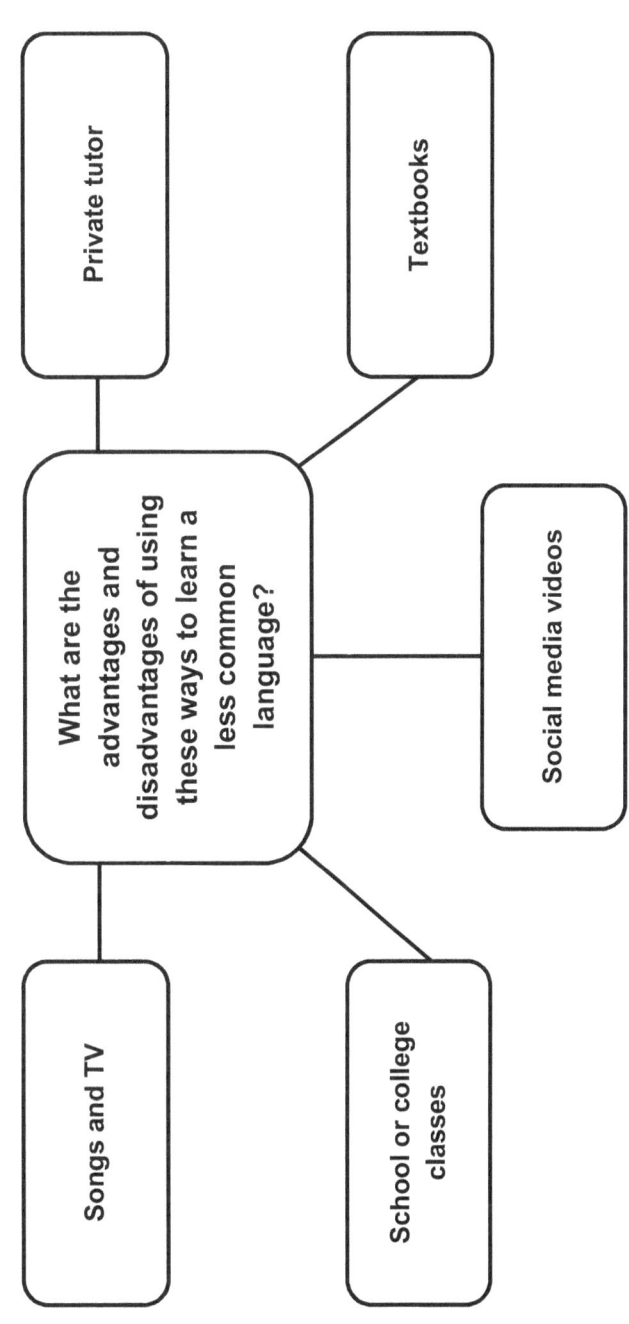

Speaking CAE   Mark sheet

Date | DD | MM | YY | Candidate _____

Marks available

Grammatical Resource	0	1	1.5	2	2.5	3	3.5	4	4.5	5
Lexical Resource	0	1	1.5	2	2.5	3	3.5	4	4.5	5
Discourse Management	0	1	1.5	2	2.5	3	3.5	4	4.5	5
Pronunciation	0	1	1.5	2	2.5	3	3.5	4	4.5	5
Interactive Communication	0	1	1.5	2	2.5	3	3.5	4	4.5	5
Global Achievement	0	1	1.5	2	2.5	3	3.5	4	4.5	5

Item descriptors

Grammatical Resource *Control* *Range*	• Degree of control of grammatical forms. • Range of grammatical forms used.
Lexical Resource *Range* *Appropriacy*	• Range of vocabulary used to give and exchange views. • Appropriacy of vocabulary used.
Discourse Management *Extent* *Relevance* *Coherence* *Cohesion*	• Stretches of language produced. • Relevance of contributions and organisation of ideas. • Use of appropriate cohesive devices and discourse markers.
Pronunciation *Intonation* *Stress* *Individual sounds*	• Intelligibility • Intonation • Word stress • Individual sounds
Interactive Communication *Initiating* *Responding* *Development*	• Initiating, responding and linking contributions to other speakers' interventions. • Maintaining and developing interaction, and negotiating towards an outcome. • Widening the scope of the interaction.

Cambridge C1 Advanced Speaking

Test 8

Test 8 – Part 1
2 minutes (3 minutes for groups of three)

Cambridge C1 Advanced: Speaking

Candidates' background

Good morning/afternoon/evening. My name is …………… and this is my colleague …………… .

And your names are?

Can I have your mark sheets, please?

Thank you.

First, we'd like to know something about you.

Select one or two questions and ask candidates in turn, as appropriate.

- **Where are you from?**
- **What do you do here/there?**
- **How long have you been studying English?**
- **What do you enjoy most about learning English?**

Select one or more questions from the following, as appropriate.

- **Which cultural tradition or festival do you most enjoy? …… (Why?)**
- **What sort of job would you like to have in the future? …… (Why?)**
- **Do you think you are good at noticing when people are lying? …… (Why? / Why not?)**
- **Do you like sharing photos on social media? …… (Why? / Why not?)**
- **Have you taken a trip recently? …… (Where?)**
- **If you had the time to take up a new hobby, what would you choose? …… (Why?)**
- **How important is it to you to have a lot of friends? …… (Why? / Why not?)**
- **Is there a subject you wish you had been able to study at school? …… (Why? / Why not?)**

Cambridge C1 Advanced: Speaking	**Test 8 – Part 2**
	4 minutes (6 minutes for groups of three)

        1 Learning practical skills   **2 Eating out**

Interlocutor   In this part of the test, I'm going to give each of you three photographs. I'd like you to talk about **two** of them on your own for about a minute, and also to answer a question about your partner's photographs.

(Candidate A), it's your turn first. Here are your photographs. They show **people learning practical skills**.

*Place **Part 2** booklet, open at **Task 1**, in front of Candidate A.*

I'd like you to compare **two** of the photographs, and say **why the people might have chosen to learn this skill, and what you think they might find challenging about learning these skills?**

All right?

Candidate A

1 minute

Interlocutor   Thank you. *(Candidate B)*, **which of these skills do you think is the most useful? …… (Why?)**

Candidate B

Approximately 30 seconds

Interlocutor   Thank you. (Can I have the booklet, please?) *Retrieve **Part 2** booklet.*

Now, *(Candidate B)*, here are your photographs. They **show people listening to music in different ways.**

*Place **Part 2** booklet, open at **Task 2**, in front of Candidate B.*

I'd like you to compare **two** of the photographs, and say **what you think the advantages of listening to music in this way might be, and how the people might be feeling**.

All right?

Candidate B

1 minute

Interlocutor   Thank you. *(Candidate A)*, **which of these situations do you think is most likely to become less popular in the future? …… (Why?)**

Candidate A

Approximately 30 seconds

Interlocutor   Thank you. (Can I have the booklet, please?) *Retrieve **Part 2** booklet.*

Test 8 – Part 2
Booklet 1

Cambridge C1 Advanced: Speaking

Why might the people have chosen to learn this skill?
What might they find challenging about learning these skills?

**What are the advantages of listening to music in these ways?
How might the people be feeling?**

Test 8 – Part 3	**Cambridge C1 Advanced: Speaking**
4 minutes (6 minutes for groups of three)	

Improving one's health and wellbeing

Interlocutor Now, I'd like you to talk about something together for about two minutes *(3 minutes for groups of three)*.

Here are some things people may prioritise when trying to improve their health and wellbeing and a question for you to discuss. First you have some time to look at the task.

Place Part 3 booklet, open at Task 3, in front of the candidates. Allow 15 seconds.

Now, talk to each other about **effective ways to achieve these goals**.

Candidates

2 minutes (3 minutes for groups of three)

Interlocutor Thank you. Now you have about a minute *(2 minutes for groups of three)* to decide **which goal is most likely to have the most significant impact on someone's health and wellbeing**.

Candidates

1 minute (2 minutes for groups of three)

Interlocutor Thank you. (Can I have the booklet, please?) *Retrieve Part 3 booklet.*

Test 8 – Part 4
5 minutes (8 minutes for groups of three)

Interlocutor *Use the following questions, in order, as appropriate:*

Do you think that people's understanding of health and wellbeing is improving? …… (Why? / Why not?)

Some people believe that social media has made made fitness more accessible; others say it is not an effective way to get fit. What do you think? …… (Why?)

Select any of the following prompts, as appropriate:
- What do you think?
- Do you agree?
- And you?

Do external feedback and comments motivate people who are trying to change their lifestyle? …… (Why? / Why not?)

What steps should employers take to improve the wellbeing of their staff? …… (Why?)

Some people say that there is a strong link between economics and health. What do you think?

In your opinion, what aspect of health and wellbeing should governments invest most in? …… (Why?)

Interlocutor Thank you. That is the end of the test.

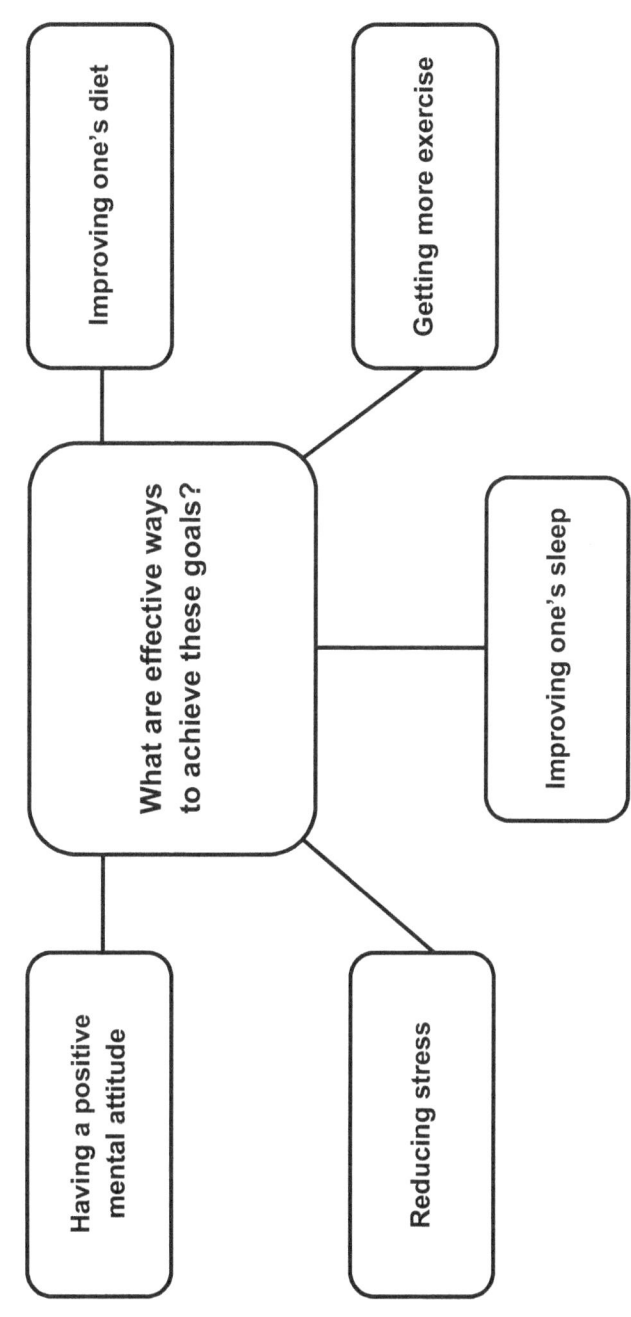

Speaking CAE — Mark sheet

Date | DD | MM | YY |

Candidate _____

Marks available

Grammatical Resource	0	1	1.5	2	2.5	3	3.5	4	4.5	5
Lexical Resource	0	1	1.5	2	2.5	3	3.5	4	4.5	5
Discourse Management	0	1	1.5	2	2.5	3	3.5	4	4.5	5
Pronunciation	0	1	1.5	2	2.5	3	3.5	4	4.5	5
Interactive Communication	0	1	1.5	2	2.5	3	3.5	4	4.5	5
Global Achievement	0	1	1.5	2	2.5	3	3.5	4	4.5	5

Item descriptors

Grammatical Resource *Control* *Range*	• Degree of control of grammatical forms. • Range of grammatical forms used.
Lexical Resource *Range* *Appropriacy*	• Range of vocabulary used to give and exchange views. • Appropriacy of vocabulary used.
Discourse Management *Extent* *Relevance* *Coherence* *Cohesion*	• Stretches of language produced. • Relevance of contributions and organisation of ideas. • Use of appropriate cohesive devices and discourse markers.
Pronunciation *Intonation* *Stress* *Individual sounds*	• Intelligibility • Intonation • Word stress • Individual sounds
Interactive Communication *Initiating* *Responding* *Development*	• Initiating, responding and linking contributions to other speakers' interventions. • Maintaining and developing interaction, and negotiating towards an outcome. • Widening the scope of the interaction.

Cambridge C1 Advanced Speaking

Test 9

Test 9 – Part 1	Cambridge C1 Advanced: Speaking
2 minutes (3 minutes for groups of three)	

Candidates' background

Good morning/afternoon/evening. My name is ………… and this is my colleague ………… .

And your names are?

Can I have your mark sheets, please?

Thank you.

First, we'd like to know something about you.

Select one or two questions and ask candidates in turn, as appropriate.

- **Where are you from?**
- **What do you do here/there?**
- **How long have you been studying English?**
- **What do you enjoy most about learning English?**

Select one or more questions from the following, as appropriate.

- **What activities do you find most useful when learning a language? …… (Why?)**
- **How would you describe your taste in clothes?**
- **What do you like to do in your favourite season? …… (Why?)**
- **Do you prefer exercising inside or outside? …… (Why?)**
- **Can you tell us about a memorable present you have given or received? …… (What?)**
- **Would you rather earn a high salary or have an interesting job? …… (Why?)**
- **How important is it to you to get on well with your neighbours? …… (Why? / Why not?)**
- **In what ways has your education influenced you as a person? …… (Why?)**

Cambridge C1 Advanced: Speaking	Test 9 – Part 2
	4 minutes (6 minutes for groups of three)

1 Forms of communication   2 Solving puzzles

Interlocutor In this part of the test, I'm going to give each of you three photographs. I'd like you to talk about **two** of them on your own for about a minute, and also to answer a question about your partner's photographs.

(Candidate A), it's your turn first. Here are your photographs. They show **people communicating in different ways**.

*Place **Part 2** booklet, open at **Task 1**, in front of Candidate A.*

I'd like you to compare **two** of the photographs, and say **why the people might be communicating in these ways, and what they need to consider when using these forms of communication**.

All right?

Candidate A

....

1 minute

Interlocutor Thank you. *(Candidate B)*, **which of these forms of communication has the greatest potential to lead to misunderstandings? …… (Why?)**

Candidate B

....

Approximately 30 seconds

Interlocutor Thank you. (Can I have the booklet, please?) *Retrieve **Part 2** booklet.*

Now, *(Candidate B)*, here are your photographs. They show **people doing different types of puzzle.**

*Place **Part 2** booklet, open at **Task 2**, in front of Candidate B.*

I'd like you to compare **two** of the photographs, and say **how the people might benefit from doing these puzzles, and what skills are necessary to do these puzzles.**

All right?

Candidate B

....

1 minute

Interlocutor Thank you. *(Candidate A)*, **which of the puzzles do you think is the most challenging? …… (Why?)**

Candidate A

....

Approximately 30 seconds

Interlocutor Thank you. (Can I have the booklet, please?) *Retrieve **Part 2** booklet.*

Test 9 – Part 2
Booklet 1

Cambridge C1 Advanced: Speaking

Why might the people be communicating in these ways?
What might they need to consider when using these forms of communication?

How might the people benefit from doing these puzzles?
What skills are necessary to do these puzzles?

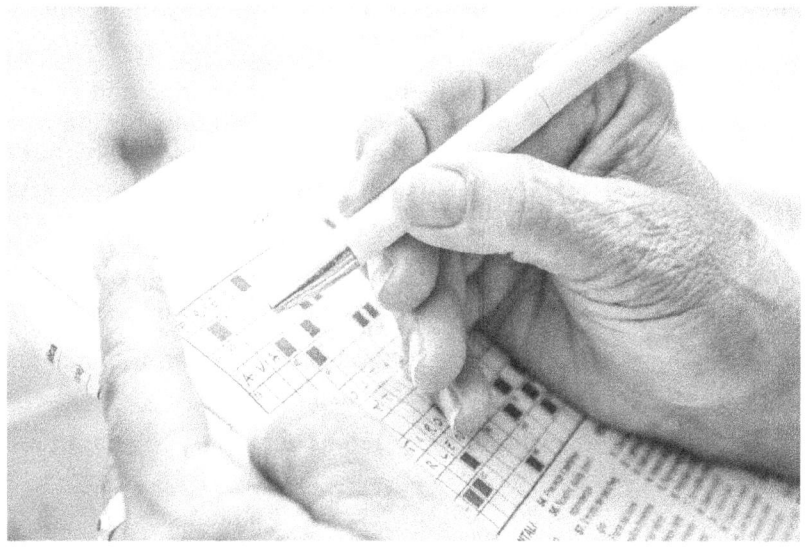

Test 9 – Part 3
4 minutes (6 minutes for groups of three)

Cambridge C1 Advanced: Speaking

Personal growth

Interlocutor   Now, I'd like you to talk about something together for about two minutes *(3 minutes for groups of three)*.

Here are some skills and qualities that employers are said to value and a question for you to discuss. First you have some time to look at the task.

*Place **Part 3** booklet, open at **Task 3**, in front of the candidates. Allow 15 seconds.*

Now, talk to each other about **how these skills and qualities could be developed in daily life.**

Candidates

2 minutes (3 minutes for groups of three)

Interlocutor   Thank you. Now you have about a minute *(2 minutes for groups of three)* to decide **which of these skills is the most useful to employers**.

Candidates

1 minute (2 minutes for groups of three)

Interlocutor   Thank you. (Can I have the booklet, please?) *Retrieve **Part 3** booklet.*

Test 9 – Part 4
5 minutes (8 minutes for groups of three)

Interlocutor   *Use the following questions, in order, as appropriate:*

Is it best for students to prioritise subjects they are interested in or ones that they think will enhance their career prospects? …… (Why?)

Some people think that universities and colleges fail to prepare students adequately for the world of work. Do you agree? …… (Why? / Why not?)

Is it a good idea to discuss personal interests and hobbies in job interviews? …… (Why? / Why not?)

Some people say that as technology advances, many of the things that employers value now will eventually be less important. What's your opinion? …… (Why?)

Do you think that perceptions of workplace skills vary from culture to culture? …… (Why? / Why not?)

To what extent should people try to adapt their personality to fit in when they are at work or school? …… (Why?)

Select any of the following prompts, as appropriate:
- **What do you think?**
- **Do you agree?**
- **And you?**

Interlocutor   Thank you. That is the end of the test.

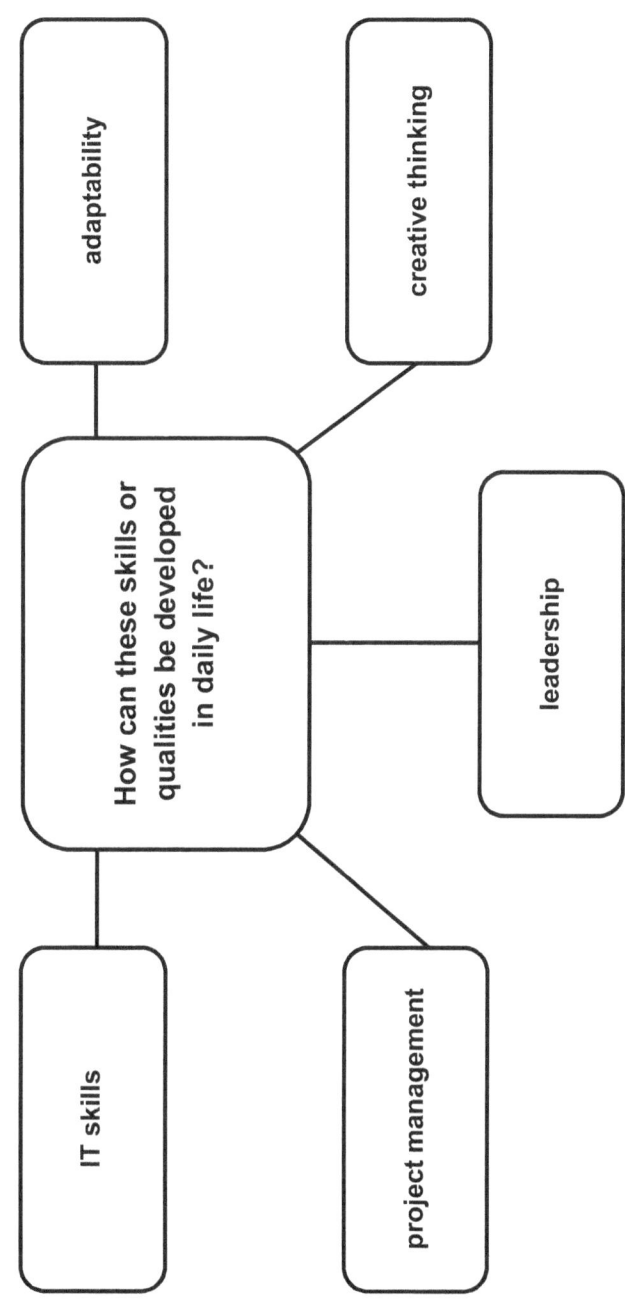

Speaking CAE — Mark sheet

Date | DD | MM | YY |

Candidate _____

Marks available

Grammatical Resource	0	1	1.5	2	2.5	3	3.5	4	4.5	5
Lexical Resource	0	1	1.5	2	2.5	3	3.5	4	4.5	5
Discourse Management	0	1	1.5	2	2.5	3	3.5	4	4.5	5
Pronunciation	0	1	1.5	2	2.5	3	3.5	4	4.5	5
Interactive Communication	0	1	1.5	2	2.5	3	3.5	4	4.5	5
Global Achievement	0	1	1.5	2	2.5	3	3.5	4	4.5	5

Item descriptors

Grammatical Resource *Control* *Range*	• Degree of control of grammatical forms. • Range of grammatical forms used.
Lexical Resource *Range* *Appropriacy*	• Range of vocabulary used to give and exchange views. • Appropriacy of vocabulary used.
Discourse Management *Extent* *Relevance* *Coherence* *Cohesion*	• Stretches of language produced. • Relevance of contributions and organisation of ideas. • Use of appropriate cohesive devices and discourse markers.
Pronunciation *Intonation* *Stress* *Individual sounds*	• Intelligibility • Intonation • Word stress • Individual sounds
Interactive Communication *Initiating* *Responding* *Development*	• Initiating, responding and linking contributions to other speakers' interventions. • Maintaining and developing interaction, and negotiating towards an outcome. • Widening the scope of the interaction.

Cambridge C1 Advanced Speaking

Test 10

Test 10 – Part 1
2 minutes (3 minutes for groups of three)

Cambridge C1 Advanced: Speaking

Candidates' background

Good morning/afternoon/evening. My name is …………… and this is my colleague …………… .

And your names are?

Can I have your mark sheets, please?

Thank you.

First, we'd like to know something about you.

Select one or two questions and ask candidates in turn, as appropriate.
•

- **Where are you from?**
- **What do you do here/there?**
- **How long have you been studying English?**
- **What do you enjoy most about learning English?**

Select one or more questions from the following, as appropriate.

- **In what ways are you a creative person? …… (Why?)**
- **What sort of changes would you like to make to your life? …… (Why?)**
- **How do you feel about meeting new people in social situations? …… (Why?)**
- **How would you describe your attitude to spending or saving money? …… (Why?)**
- **Could you tell us about a risk you have taken in your life?**
- **If you could learn to play a musical instrument, what would you pick? …… (Why?)**
- **How important is it to you to keep up with popular TV shows? …… (Why? / Why not?)**
- **What is your favourite memory from your childhood or schooldays? …… (Why?)**

Cambridge C1 Advanced: Speaking	Test 10 – Part 2
	4 minutes (6 minutes for groups of three)

1 Giving opinions **2 Advertising**

Interlocutor In this part of the test, I'm going to give each of you three photographs. I'd like you to talk about **two** of them on your own for about a minute, and also to answer a question about your partner's photographs.

(Candidate A), it's your turn first. Here are your photographs. They show **situations where people are giving opinions.**

*Place **Part 2** booklet, open at **Task 1**, in front of Candidate A.*

I'd like you to compare **two** of the photographs, and say **what might make the people reluctant to give their opinions, and how the people are feeling**.

All right?

Candidate A

1 minute

Interlocutor Thank you. *(Candidate B)*, **in which of these situations is it most important to be honest about what you think? …… (Why?)**

Candidate B

Approximately 30 seconds

Interlocutor Thank you. (Can I have the booklet, please?) *Retrieve **Part 2** booklet.*

Now, *(Candidate B)*, here are your photographs. They show **people using different methods to sell something.**

*Place **Part 2** booklet, open at **Task 2**, in front of Candidate B.*

I'd like you to compare **two** of the photographs, and say **what might the people might like about using these methods, and what they need to do in these situations**.

All right?

Candidate B

1 minute

Interlocutor Thank you. *(Candidate A)*, **which of these methods is likely to require the most preparation? …… (Why?)**

Candidate A

Approximately 30 seconds

Interlocutor Thank you. (Can I have the booklet, please?) *Retrieve **Part 2** booklet.*

Test 10 – Part 2
Booklet 1

Cambridge C1 Advanced: Speaking

Why might the people be reluctant to give their opinions in these situations?
How might the people be feeling?

What might the people like about using these methods?
What do they need to do in these situations?

Test 10 – Part 3	**Cambridge C1 Advanced: Speaking**
4 minutes (6 minutes for groups of three)	

Perks

Interlocutor Now, I'd like you to talk about something together for about two minutes *(3 minutes for groups of three).*

Here are some additional benefits that some companies offer as well as salaries and a question for you to discuss. First you have some time to look at the task.

Place Part 3 booklet, open at Task 3, in front of the candidates. Allow 15 seconds.

Now, talk to each other about **how important these perks are to employees.**

Candidates

....

2 minutes (3 minutes for groups of three)

Interlocutor Thank you. Now you have about a minute *(2 minutes for groups of three)* to decide **which perk is most likely to influence people's perceptions of the company**.

Candidates

....

1 minute (2 minutes for groups of three)

Interlocutor Thank you. (Can I have the booklet, please?) *Retrieve Part 3 booklet.*

Test 10 – Part 4
5 minutes (8 minutes for groups of three)

Interlocutor *Use the following questions, in order, as appropriate:* | *Select any of the following prompts, as appropriate:*
- What do you think?
- Do you agree?
- And you?

Is it better to stay with one employer for a long time or change companies often throughout one's career? …… (Why?)

Some people believe that companies that offer social activities for their staff are more successful. Do you agree? …… (Why? / Why not?)

Would you agree that jobseekers expect more from employers nowadays? …… (Why? / Why not?)

Some people say that staff loyalty is an old-fashioned concept. What do you think?

Is it acceptable for companies to link people's salaries to their work performance? …… (Why? / Why not?)

What questions should jobseekers ask potential employers during job interviews? …… (Why? / Why not?)

Interlocutor Thank you. That is the end of the test.

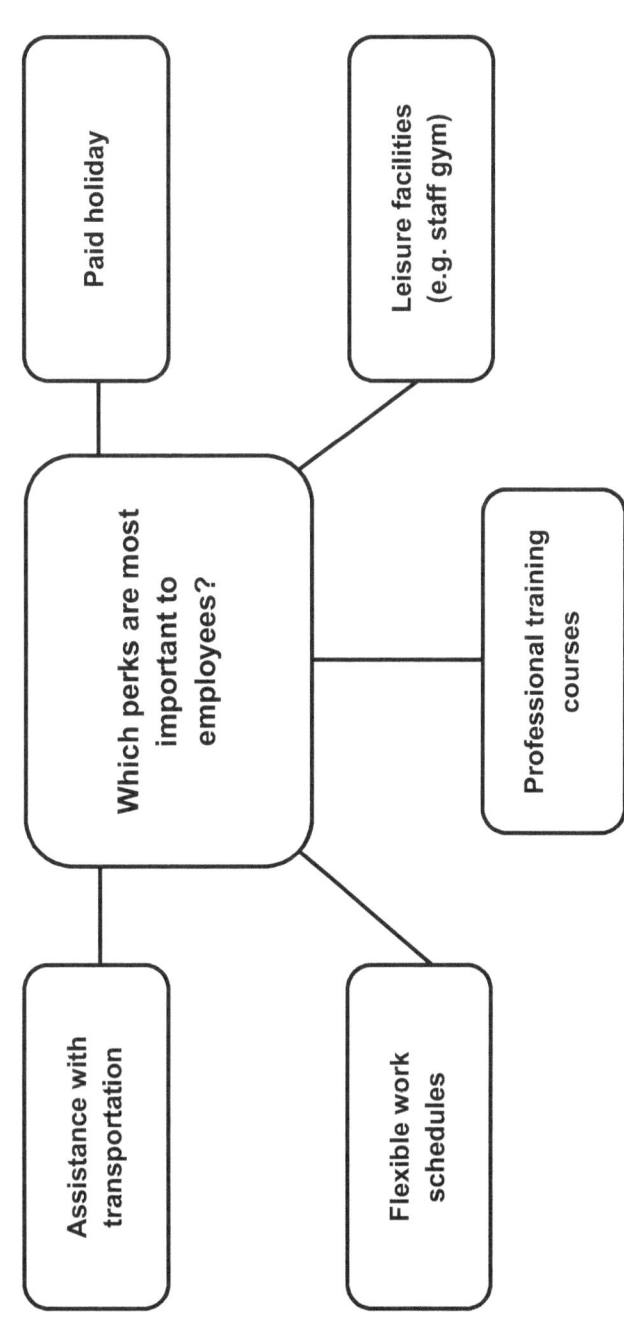

Speaking CAE — Mark sheet

Date | DD | MM | YY |

Candidate _____

Marks available

Grammatical Resource	0	1	1.5	2	2.5	3	3.5	4	4.5	5
Lexical Resource	0	1	1.5	2	2.5	3	3.5	4	4.5	5
Discourse Management	0	1	1.5	2	2.5	3	3.5	4	4.5	5
Pronunciation	0	1	1.5	2	2.5	3	3.5	4	4.5	5
Interactive Communication	0	1	1.5	2	2.5	3	3.5	4	4.5	5
Global Achievement	0	1	1.5	2	2.5	3	3.5	4	4.5	5

Item descriptors

Grammatical Resource *Control* *Range*	• Degree of control of grammatical forms. • Range of grammatical forms used.
Lexical Resource *Range* *Appropriacy*	• Range of vocabulary used to give and exchange views. • Appropriacy of vocabulary used.
Discourse Management *Extent* *Relevance* *Coherence* *Cohesion*	• Stretches of language produced. • Relevance of contributions and organisation of ideas. • Use of appropriate cohesive devices and discourse markers.
Pronunciation *Intonation* *Stress* *Individual sounds*	• Intelligibility • Intonation • Word stress • Individual sounds
Interactive Communication *Initiating* *Responding* *Development*	• Initiating, responding and linking contributions to other speakers' interventions. • Maintaining and developing interaction, and negotiating towards an outcome. • Widening the scope of the interaction.

Model answers

Test 1

Speaking CAE

Model answers – Test 1

The C1 Advanced examination is usually taken by candidates who want to obtain a C1-level certificate, which generally corresponds to a native-like level of English.

As described by the Common European Framework of Reference for Languages (CEFRL), candidates with a C1 level are considered to be *proficient users*, that is, users who show *mastery* or *comprehensive operational proficiency* of the English language, thus being able to:

- understand with ease virtually everything heard or read
- summarise information from different spoken and written sources, reconstructing arguments and accounts in a coherent presentation
- express themselves spontaneously, fluently and precisely, discerning finer shades of meaning even in more complex situations.

The purpose of the following model answers is to provide teachers and candidates with an example of language production and test performance that would score a high mark in a real C1 Advanced Speaking test.

These answers contain grammatical and lexical features as well as a range of discourse resources suited to an advanced level of English.

Please note that a high level of linguistic accuracy is expected at C1 level.

On pages 96–100, there are comments highlighting different aspects of the model answers, such as:

- the strategies candidates make use of to address some of the parts
- the ways in which candidates express their opinions
- how candidates interact with one another, etc.

The aim of these comments is to draw the reader's attention to important details that might help them to achieve a successful performance in this part of the C1 Advanced examination.

While reading the model answers and the examiner's comments, please bear in mind the following:

- The test is taken in pairs (or trios), and candidates are expected to interact with each other.
- The approximate timing of each part of the test is as follows:
    - Part 1: 2 minutes (pair) / 3 minutes (trio)
    - Part 2: 4 minutes (pair) / 6 minutes (trio)
    - Part 3: 4 minutes (pair) / 6 minutes (trio)
    - Part 4: 5 minutes (pair) / 8 minutes (trio)
- These model answers would achieve a high score in a C1 Advanced Speaking test, and so should be regarded as strong-performance answers that provide examples of the types of linguistic structures candidates are expected to produce at this level rather than examples of minimum performance to pass.

Test 1 – Part 1 – Model answers

Interlocutor	Where are you from, Candidate A?
Candidate A	*I'm from Bursa, in the north west of Turkey.*
Interlocutor	And you, Candidate B?
Candidate B	*I'm also Turkish but I'm from Antalya, which is on the south coast.*
Interlocutor	Are you working or studying at the moment?
Candidate B	*I'm at university. I'm in the second year of my law degree at Istanbul University.*
Interlocutor	And you?
Candidate A	*Well, I've got the best of both worlds, as I'm working part-time in my parents' restaurant while I'm doing my business management degree.*
Interlocutor	Would you describe yourself as an optimistic person?
Candidate A	*That's not something I've ever really considered before, actually. But by and large, I'm a "glass-half-full" sort of person! What I mean is that I'm usually able to find a way to look on the bright side. Or at the very least, I try not to dwell on the negatives which amounts to the same thing, I guess.*
Interlocutor	How important is it to you to keep up with the latest trends?
Candidate B	*If you're referring to the fads or crazes that pop up on social media, then no. Most of that stuff passes me by, but I'm more interested in tech innovations. For instance, every now and then a gadget like smartwatch comes along that's a total gamechanger, so I like trying to predict the next big thing.*
Interlocutor	Thank you.

Test 1 – Part 2 – Model answers

Being active

Task 1 – Long turn

Interlocutor	In this part of the test, I'm going to give each of you three photographs. I'd like you to talk about **two** of them on your own for about a minute, and also to answer questions about your partner's photographs. *(Candidate A)* It's your turn first. Here are your photographs (A – people hiking; B – people doing yoga; C – girls playing football). They show people being active. I'd like you to compare **two** of the photos, and say what you think the people in these photos are enjoying about being active, and how these activities can help them in their daily lives. All right?
Candidate A	*OK, well, I'm immediately drawn to the photo with the people hiking. It's a great illustration of the mental benefits of being active. What I mean is that in this picture, it looks like a fairly strenuous trail, which is of course physically tiring, but at the same time, I'm sure the hikers must be enjoying the challenge. I doubt you'd get that same feeling of accomplishment in the other photo. You don't know what you can achieve, until you give it a try. That's a valuable lesson to bring into your work or studies. And of course, spending time in the great outdoors is a mood booster. But if we're talking about feeling good, then I think that's where the picture of the team game wins hands down. You can see that the girls in the photo are having a lot of fun, and this photo definitely conveys more of a sense of enjoyment than the hiking photo. Team sports are so enjoyable because you're working together and motivating each other. You can definitely reap the benefits of that in work or study contexts because these often involve group situations.*

Speaking CAE

Interlocutor	Thank you. (Candidate B), what is the main factor that encourages people to be active?
Candidate B	*Well, it's interesting that (Candidate A) has referred mainly to the psychological and mental benefits of being active. I completely agree, but I suspect that's not the main reason people want to be active. If I'm being brutally honest, it's about improving the way they look, or at least it is for a lot of my peers. I'm not saying people only exercise out of vanity, but it's probably the main driver.*
Interlocutor	Thank you. (*Can I have the booklet, please?*) Now, (*Candidate B*), here are your photographs. They show people doing different types of shopping (photo A. woman using a tablet to shop, photo B a family shopping at the supermarket, photo C – people in an outdoor market) I'd like you to compare **two** of the photographs, and say why you think the people have chosen to shop in these ways, and what people should consider when shopping in these ways. All right?
Candidate B	*I think I'll compare the supermarket and online retail pictures. Looking at the supermarket photo, we immediately see the social aspect of shopping which is something which you don't get from websites. The family probably could have got the items delivered, but going out and choosing what to buy together might make it more of a fun occasion. As supermarkets tend to be near other amenities, they might have combined the trip with other activities like a trip to the cinema. The other major plus for shoppers is being able to see the products, smell them, and judge the quality. Stores try their best to tempt you with eye-catching displays or special promotions, don't they? In my opinion, you can easily end up making impulse buys, so that's something to think about if you want to stick to a budget. Making a clear shopping list is one way to avoid temptation, I think. Moving on to the woman shopping from her tablet, well, this type of retail is about convenience. You can do it all with one click or swipe without having to go out. By contrast, a trip to the shops involves finding the right products, waiting in queues, loading the shopping and then getting home. And of course, the woman in the photo might not live near shops or have a vehicle. However, the key thing to think about is your online security. Sadly, it's vital to think about who can see your card details, and take steps to prevent any possibility of financial fraud.*
Interlocutor	Thank you. (*Candidate A*), which of these types of shopping is the most convenient?
Candidate A	*Well, it depends on your location and access to transport, but in most cases, supermarket shopping. You can go when you want, and you don't have to worry about whether the company will deliver the right product, or make a mistake with the order. It's also easier to return items if you're not satisfied.*
Interlocutor	Thank you. (*Can I have the booklet, please?*)

Test 1 – Part 3 – Model answers

Trying to help society

Collaborative task

Interlocutor	Now, I'd like you to talk about something together for about **two** minutes. Here are some ways that people sometimes choose to try and help society and a question for you to discuss. First you have some time to look at the task. Now, talk to each other about what might make someone reluctant to try these ways of helping society.
Candidate A	*Let's see... well, not everyone has the resources to be able to donate to charity, do they? And even if they can afford to make the occasional donation, they might hesitate on the grounds that their small individual donation probably won't have much impact.*
Candidate B	*Oh yes, that's right, and that's why people often feel powerless and frustrated. It's the same when it comes to environmental issues. The sheer scale of the problem can seem so overwhelming that*

Model answers

	there's the assumption that you can't make a difference. That's why for me, politics is the key to improving society. It's sort of why I got into law. What do you think?
Candidate A	*Well, I'm in two minds, really. I mean it's all very well wanting to get into politics in order to change things, as you say. But let's be honest, it's easier said than done. Unless you have the right connections, and background, you might feel like you simply don't belong in that world. You might not even get a foot in the door. But that's not to say that I think people shouldn't try.*
Candidate B	*I see what you mean. So it sounds like you think people prefer to take smaller-scale actions instead, maybe like community projects?*
Candidate A	*Yes, but if we're being asked to talk about why people are hesitant to get involved, there are still plenty of things that might put them off. For example, community projects can be very difficult to organise. You might start out with great enthusiasm, but before you know it, everyone's interest has waned, and the project has stalled.*
Candidate B	*That's true. And I suppose in some places, people might not be planning to settle down in that community for a long time so they might not see the point in getting involved. It's a pity, though, to put it mildly.*
Candidate A	*So do you think that's why people might not feel compelled to help their neighbours out?*
Candidate B	*I'm not sure. That might be part of it. Sadly, these days you don't necessarily know your neighbours by name so you might not feel comfortable asking for or offering help. What's your take?*
Candidate A	*Indeed. I'd go along with that. You might not even know the neighbour's in need, or you just think that they already have support from friends and family.*
Candidate B	*Yes, so that leaves us with sharing information. Do you think this means education?*
Candidate A	*Possibly, although I interpreted it as sharing information online, for example on social media. And I know personally, I don't feel comfortable doing that.*
Candidate B	*I don't have an issue with it, but I can see why people might not want to feel like they're coming across as patronising or maybe even obsessive.*
Candidate A	*Exactly, and at the same time, you might assume what you want to share is already common knowledge.*
Interlocutor	Thank you. Now you have about a minute to decide which way is most likely to make a difference to society.
Candidate B	*Well, we've already touched on it, but I'm still inclined to believe that politics will have the biggest impact. As far as I'm concerned, you need to start with legislation if you really want to change the world.*
Candidate A	*I see what you're saying and there's an argument for that if we're talking about issues such as the economy or climate change. But if politicians and governments are dealing with major problems, isn't there a danger that they become out of touch with what's happening in local communities?*
Candidate B	*Hmmm... I hadn't thought about it from that perspective. Yes, I suppose the benefit of focusing on local issues is that there's more likely to be a specific outcome that people can see and appreciate. It sort of goes back to your point about the importance of being personally invested. Would you agree?*
Candidate A	*Absolutely, and not to mention the fact that local people are in the best position to understand what's happening in the community, what people need, and how to help them. It's as rewarding as helping a neighbour in need but on a wider scale.*
Candidate B	*Good point. And I'd argue that's better than donating money to charity. When you do that, you can never be sure where your money is going, what is being used for, or whether it's making any difference at all. And I don't think you're keen on sharing information about an issue, are you?*
Candidate A	*Don't get me wrong, education is important. If you can easily inform people about an issue, that's great, but I don't think it's as effective as getting involved in local community work.*

Speaking CAE

Candidate B I couldn't agree more. I think that settles it. Community work should come first.

Interlocutor Thank you. (*Can I have the booklet, please?*)

Test 1 – Part 4 – Model answers

Question-based discussion

Interlocutor Do you think everyone has a role to play in society?

Candidate A Yes, I do. I mean, as we saw with all the activities we've just discussed, there are plenty of ways to use your talents to help society. Everyone has something to offer.

Candidate B I couldn't have put it better myself, really. It doesn't matter whether you're a human rights lawyer or a parent teaching their children to be kind and respectful, we all depend on one another.

Candidate A That's right, so we can't just say "oh, that's someone else's responsibility".

Interlocutor Some people believe that smaller, local charities achieve more than national charities. Do you agree?

Candidate B It's an interesting question, because when I think of the charity sector, I immediately imagine large organisations. The thing is, national charities can invest more in their marketing, and because of that, they reach more donors. From that perspective, smaller charities are never going to be able to compete, are they?

Candidate A Mmm.. but do you think getting lots of donations is the same thing as making a difference? To me, I don't know if that makes them more effective in terms of having an actual impact, or just better at fundraising.

Candidate B Yes, that's what makes the question hard to answer. I guess it's related to what we've been discussing. Local charities are similar to local community groups. I think they can achieve more in terms of getting things done, if we're talking about small-scale projects because they can respond more quickly. But we still need national charities for the most serious issues or the ones that need specialist expertise.

Candidate A Especially in the case of things like diseases or environmental causes.

Interlocutor Do you believe that most people go into politics for the right reasons?

Candidate B Obviously, politicians don't always have the best reputation but I'd like to think most people go into politics to improve society. There will always be some corrupt politicians but I think that's the minority. It's just that they're the ones that get the attention in the media.

Interlocutor (*Candidate A*), what about you?

Candidate A I'm not sure really. Yes, they probably start out thinking they can make a difference, but once you get a bit of power, it's probably very different. You have to take actions you secretly don't agree with, or make compromises just to stay popular with voters.

Candidate B That's inevitable to a certain degree, I guess. But it seems we both think politicians have good intentions at the start, so that's something, I suppose!

Interlocutor Some people say the idea of 'community' is disappearing in many places. What do you think?

Candidate A In my opinion it is because we don't have the same close relationships with people in our neighbourhoods nowadays. I don't just mean the people who live in the same street or building. Where are the local shops? Local cafes? If we don't have a local community, it's hardly surprising that we don't help each other.

Candidate B	*Hmmm. I have to say, I'm a little less pessimistic on this issue. I do think you're right in that local neighbourhoods are changing and we're losing that human interaction. Even so, I see it in a different way because there's a really thriving online community of people all around the world. These people share ideas and help each other. It might be online, but it still counts.*
Interlocutor	Do you think social media has a largely positive or negative impact on society?
Candidate A	*Well, as (Candidate B) has just mentioned, social media can be used in beneficial ways. For instance, it can certainly bring cultures together and promote greater understanding. I think breaking down barriers to information is extremely important because that is how society develops, but I still worry about the negative sides. For instance, it can seem very superficial at times.*
Interlocutor	*(Candidate B)*, do you agree?
Candidate B	*Yes, I think so because having access to diverse views is vital. I also agree about the negative side. It tends to make people focus on how they're coming across, on how popular they are. When people are too obsessed with that, it can really affect their mental health and self-esteem.*
Interlocutor	Some people say that it is the responsibility of governments, not charities to help society. What's your opinion?
Candidate B	*It's hard to answer that if I'm being honest. If governments had unlimited time, resources, and expertise, then yes, we wouldn't need charities, but that's never going to happen. The reality is that we need both. In fact, charities will always be needed because they're often the organisations that guide governments and shine light on what needs to be done, and why.*
Candidate A	*You mean in terms of their campaigns? That's a really interesting point and you're right about that because charities can influence government policy. As far as I'm concerned though, governments should be leading the way in terms of shaping society, which I think is what the question is really getting at. Charities should be there to provide additional support. The problem comes when governments neglect their responsibilities so it rests solely on the shoulders of charities instead.*
Candidate B	*Yes, you've hit the nail on the head, there.*
Interlocutor	Thank you. That is the end of the test.

Examiner comments

Test 1

Speaking CPE

Examiner comments

Test 1 – Part 1 – Model answers

In Part 1, candidates are asked about themselves, their background and experiences. These questions are scripted, and the interlocutor will never improvise them. Candidates are expected to answer and justify their responses, but these should not turn into a long monologue. If the answer given to a question is particularly short, the examiner will probably ask a follow-up question such as "Why?" or "Why not?".

Therefore, candidates should answer more than a simple "Yes", "No" or one-word answer, but not much more.

For example:

Question	Are you working or studying at the moment?
Answer	Well, I've got the best of both worlds, as I'm working part-time in my parents' restaurant while I'm doing my business management degree.

Given the nature of the conversation, these answers should sound natural and non-rehearsed. Sounding natural is part of being fluent in a language, so using some informal expressions (*pretty sure*), exclamations (*Fingers crossed!*), contractions (*I'm, don't*) or discourse markers *(Well)* is actually encouraged, as long as they are natural and not used excessively.

As this is a C1-level speaking test, candidates' answers should show C1-level grammar and vocabulary, even in Part 1, if possible. For this reason, in the model answers provided for Part 1, there are some appropriate C1-level phrases like:

- *by and large*
- *every now and then*
- *have the best of both worlds*
- *look on the bright side*

- *which amounts to the same thing*
- *try not to dwell on*
- *at the very least*
- *tech innovations*

Part 1 is probably not the most suitable part for candidates to prove their level, but they should still try to show what they know, and, above all, try to sound natural.

Key things to practise:

- Talking about personal background referring to past, present and future situations
- Providing brief examples to illustrate points (e.g. *for instance…like the smartwatch*)
- Using phrases to clarify meaning or to add precision (e.g. *if you're referring to…what I mean is that*)

Test 1 – Part 2 – Model answers

As with Part 1, the focus of Part 2 is individual speaking. Each candidate is asked to compare two pictures (which they choose from a set of three) and answer two questions about them, in an individual long turn of one minute without interruption. This is a chance for candidates to show how well they can speak on their own in a longer turn. Candidates' grammar and vocabulary are expected to be excellent and, more specifically in this part, there is special emphasis on their discourse management – i.e. how long they can speak for (*extent*), how relevant their contributions (*relevance*) are, and how well they can organise and connect their speech (*coherence* and *cohesion*).

Please note that it is common for candidates to be interrupted when the time is up. However, this will not affect the candidate's mark negatively, as long as what he/she has said has been delivered using C1-level grammar and vocabulary in a well-organised speech.

Notice the following elements in the sample answers on pages 89–93:

The language candidates use

If we take a look at Candidate A's and Candidate B's turns, we notice that they:

- **use appropriate C1 grammar and lexis:** *I'm immediately drawn to…it's a great illustration of…reap the benefits…looks fairly strenuous…sense of accomplishment…the great outdoors…convey…other amenities…making impulse buys…any possibility of financial fraud…eye-catching displays…wins hands down…retail…etc.*

- **use cohesive devices and discourse markers to organise his/her speech:** *If we're talking about…looking at the supermarket photo…but at the same time…moving on to the woman shopping from her tablet…the other major plus…However…etc.*

- **compares, speculates and offer opinions when referring to the pictures:** *it's a great illustration of…I'm sure the hikers must be enjoying…I doubt you'd get…I think that's where the picture of the team game wins hands down…this photo definitely conveys more of a sense of enjoyment than the hiking photo…the family probably could have got the items delivered…in my opinion…etc.*

These expressions show that candidates are capable of responding to visual stimuli to discuss broader themes using a range of language functions while talking at length.

Follow-up question

After the individual turn, the interlocutor will ask the other candidate a question related to the topic their partner has just been discussing. The candidate should answer this question in about thirty seconds.

This question will not require the candidate to refer specifically to their partner's pictures. However, candidates may decide to comment on ideas that have already been mentioned by their partner.

Note how Candidate B does this when asked a follow-up question about Candidate's A monologue about being physically active:

- ***Well, it's interesting that (Candidate A) has referred mainly to the psychological and mental benefits of being active. I completely agree, but*** *I suspect that's not the main reason people want to be active. If I'm being brutally honest, it's about improving the way they look, or at least it is for a lot of my peers. I'm not saying people only exercise out of sheer vanity, but it's probably the main driver.*

Key things to practise:

- Making the connection between an image and a general topic (e.g. *It's a great illustration of the mental benefits of being active…*)
- Justifying ideas (e.g. *You can definitely reap the benefits of that in work or study contexts because these often involve group situations.*)

Speaking CPE

Test 1 – Part 3 – Model answers

In Part 3, candidates work together on a collaborative task. The candidates are presented with a booklet showing a question and some written prompts that serve as ideas for the discussion. Candidates discuss the question and prompts for two minutes. The candidates are then asked a further question which requires the candidates to reach a decision. Candidates discuss this question for one minute.

The main focus of this part of the test is interactive communication, so there is special emphasis on assessing skills, such as providing and eliciting opinions and reactions, evaluating, negotiating, and so on. Candidates need to demonstrate turn-taking skills and the ability to respond to each other.

Notice the following elements in the sample answers on pages 89–93:

The language candidates use

If we take a look at the candidates' model answers, we notice that they:

- **use appropriate C1 grammar and lexis:** *on the grounds that…feel powerless and frustrated…when it comes to…sheer scale…overwhelming…assumption…in two minds…it's all very well…easier said than done…hesitant to…before you know it…waned…has stalled…feel compelled to…settle down…to put it mildly…interpreted it as…come across as…obsessive…personally invested in…rewarding…that settles it…come first…etc.*

- **express views and opinions:** *That's why for me…I'm in two minds…I mean…let's be honest…that's not to say I think…I suppose…I'm not sure…I don't have an issue with it…I'm still inclined to believe that…as far as I'm concerned…yes but if we're being asked to talk about…I suppose…I'd argue that…you can never be sure…don't get me wrong…etc.*

- **agree and disagree:** *Oh yes, that's right…I see what you mean…that's true…indeed…I'd go along with that…exactly…I hadn't though about it from that perspective…absolutely…good point…I couldn't agree more…I think that settles it…etc.*

- **employ turn-taking gambits:** *do they?…what do you think?…So it sounds like you're saying…do you think that's why…?…what's your take?…do you think this means…?…isn't there a danger that…?…would you agree?…are you?…etc.*

These expressions show that candidates are capable of initiating, responding and linking contributions to each other's turn, and that they can develop a successful interaction and negotiate towards an outcome in a very natural way.

In this case, both candidates reach an agreement by the end. However, this is by no means a test requirement and candidates' marks will not be affected by whether an agreement or conclusion is reached or not.

Finally, it is extremely important that this part does not turn into two separate, individual turns at speaking rather than a seamless interaction. Therefore, candidates should avoid lengthy answers and should try to involve their partner at the end of each turn to keep the conversation flowing.

Key things to practise:

- Linking to and building on the partner's turn by referring to their ideas (e.g. *as you say…we've already touched on it but…it sort of goes back to your point about…and I don't think you're keen on…are you?…etc.*)

Examiner comments

Test 1 – Part 4 – Model answers

Part 4 builds on the discussion topic explored in part 3. The examiner asks a series of discussion questions which the candidates are expected to develop using a range of communicative and interactive strategies (such as those demonstrated in Part 3).

The examiner may invite one of the candidates to comment on what their partner (e.g. *do you agree?*).

As with previous parts of the test, candidates are advised to show that they are paying attention to what their partner is saying. This will enable them to link ideas well.

Candidates' interaction

Here (page 92) we see great examples of interaction, linguistic proficiency and insightful responses:

Interlocutor	*Some people say that the idea of 'community' is disappearing in many places. What do you think?*
Candidate A	*In my opinion it is because we don't have the same close relationships with people in our neighbourhoods nowadays. I don't just mean the people who live in the same street or building. Where are the local shops? Local cafes? If we don't have a local community, it's hardly surprising that we don't help each other.*
Candidate B	*Hmmm. I have to say, I'm little less pessimistic on this issue. I do think you're right in that local neighbourhoods are changing and we're losing that human interaction. Even so, I see it in a different way because there's a really thriving online community of people all around the world. These people share ideas and help each other. It might be online, but it still counts.*

Candidate A provides a clear answer to the question but develops it further by providing their interpretation of the question. (I don't just mean the people who... where are the local cafes?) He/she then explains how this interpretation relates to the interlocutor's question (*If we don't... it's hardly surprising that...*). This shows that the candidate can support their ideas and develop a line of argument. Candidate B responds by highlighting how his/her stance differs from his/her partner's (*I have to say, I'm a little less pessimistic on this issue ... even so*) and where they agree (*I do think you're right in that ...*) They justify why they believe their argument is valid, and shows awareness of why some people might not agree (*It might be online, but it still counts*).

The following example (page 93) also shows some great interaction in Part 3:

Interlocutor	*Some people say that it is the responsibility of governments, not charities to help society. What's your opinion?*
Candidate B	*It's hard to answer that if I'm being honest. If governments had unlimited time, resources, and expertise, then yes, we wouldn't need charities, but that's never going to happen. The reality is that we need both. In fact, charities will always be needed because they're often the organisations that guide governments and shine light on what needs to be done, and why.*
Candidate A	*You mean in terms of their campaigns? That's a really interesting point and you're right about that because charities can influence government policy. As far as I'm concerned though, governments should be leading the way in terms of shaping society, which I think is what the question is really getting at. Charities should be there to provide additional support. The problem comes when governments neglect their duties so it rests solely on the shoulders of charities instead.*
Candidate B	*Yes, you've hit the nail on the head there.*

Candidate B starts by using a filler phrase to get more thinking time (*It's hard to answer that, if I'm being honest,...*) and then highlights a situation in which an answer would be easier to find (*If governments had unlimited... then yes...*) before explaining why the real answer is more nuanced. This gives him/her the chance to reframe the topic in a way that they can develop using idiomatic language (*charities will always be needed because they're often the organisations that guide governments and shine a light on...*).

Candidate A uses a different reframing technique, by offering a clarification on what Candidate B has just said (*You mean in terms of their campaigns?*). Not only does this enable Candidate A to show that he/she is paying attention to their partner, but it gives them an opportunity to build on that idea (*That's a really interesting point and you're right about that because charities can influence government policy*). He/she then uses a refocusing phrase to direct the discussion back to the original question (*which I think is what the question is really getting at*) before developing the response (*Charities should be there to provide additional support. The problem comes when governments neglect their duties*) and with idiomatic language (*so it rests solely on the shoulders of charities*).

Key things to practise:

- Framing a subject or question (e.g. *When I think of…I immediately imagine…if we're talking about…do you mean…in terms of…*)

Throughout the sample answers provided by candidates in every part of the test, we can see that they:

- use C1-level structures
- sound very natural
- are well connected and organised
- tend to end with a question for the other candidate, which keeps the discussion going.

Finally, it is worth mentioning the presence of collocations, idiomatic expressions and phrasal verbs typical of a proficient level of English. For example:

Best of both worlds…rest on the shoulders of…get a foot in the door…start out…break down barriers…glass half-full, etc.

At this level, candidates would be expected to use some examples of this type of language to add colour to their speech, although with less frequency than at C2 level.

www.ingramcontent.com/pod-product-compliance
Lightning Source LLC
Chambersburg PA
CBHW081918090526
44590CB00019B/3404